A SHAMANIC KUNDALINI AWAKENING

Brendan Ring

CONTENTS

PREFACE

This is the story of my journey from separation, to reconnection with the universe. It is unusual in that there are two interlocking streams within the process, kundalini awakening *and* shamanic awakening. Although these processes are natural and the most ancient forms of spiritual phenomena experienced by human beings, neither are accepted or acknowledged by western science or culture. Anthropology has viewed shamans as schizophrenics and scholars have viewed kundalini, as described in the ancient yogic texts, as little more than a beautiful metaphor. Yet these are very real processes, not confined to man-made parameters and may happen to any of us, irrespective of race or cultural background.

My journey began with yoga and that tradition holds that we pick up spiritually in the next life, from the point we reached in the previous one. As a child I was drawn into advanced yogic practices. After a break of many years I returned to yoga in adult life, receiving the great gift of a kundalini awakening. After some years within the kundalini awakening process I began to realise that a great deal of the phenomena I was experiencing fell firmly within the realms of shamanism, as well as yoga. This was in fact first noticed by my wife Michèle, who strongly intuited that there was a shamanic element to what was happening to me. Initially, I firmly rejected this possibility. I didn't really know what shamanism was, I had a prejudiced opinion based on uneducated preconceptions and had absolutely no desire or ambition in that direction. Eventually, the shamanic nature of the phenomena I was experiencing became so strong that I began to seriously consider that she may have been right all along. Searching for answers I began to come across accounts both old and new, which closely corroborated my experiences as being shamanic initiations.

Awareness of kundalini awakening has increased due to the spreading of yoga in the west and the rise of the Internet, but shamanic awakenings still remain largely a mystery, even in spiritual circles. As with kundalini awakenings, each individual shamanic awakening will be different and I'm not suggesting that what I relate in the narrative is the only way.

What is described here is a shamanic path of consciousness, a sort of 'yoga of shamanism'.

I term what I have experienced, a shamanic kundalini awakening. A shamanic enlightenment process, where the universe expresses itself primarily through the consciousnesses of animals, trees, plants and stones. An experiential animism based in the direct revelation, that what we call 'god' is in nature and that in spite of everything we have done and are doing to the planet, nature is still willing to talk to us.

This is not a 'how to' book, there are numerous others out there offering practical advice concerning kundalini and shamanism. Nor is this book connected to any commercial spiritual organisation, there are no courses attached, it promotes no systems, you won't find workshops with me, advertised at the back. I make no claims to be a yogi, shaman, guru or spiritual teacher, this is simply a sharing of a deeply personal on-going spiritual awakening. I share purely in the hope that those experiencing similar phenomena might gain something from my own account and know they are not alone.

I dedicate this book to Michèle, who accepted without question the validity of the spiritual experiences I describe and fully supported the on-going process of transformation they initiated. It is a rare soul that can do this.

Thanks also, to Marjolaine and Éimhín, for their support and understanding.

Special thanks to

Susan Ferguson, Dawn Dancing Otter, Josephine Fire Lame Deer and the late Martin A. Egan.

CHAPTER ONE

CUMHA

I used to think it all began the night I dreamed of the goddess Isis. In the dream I was walking the land around my house; there are thick, drystone walls everywhere and hidden inside one of these I found a tiny statue of Isis. It was pure white, very simple in design and beautiful. I brought it back to the house where a huge vat of water was waiting. I placed it in the water and Isis grew to full size and floated to the top. This dream felt so real that the next day I actually went looking for the statue. I didn't find it but it may well be there. Here, in the south west of France, in the land of Cathars and Templars, the black Madonnas are still to be seen and many believe that originally they were representations of this Egyptian goddess of rebirth. The next night, I again dreamed of a goddess. This time I saw a beautiful woman standing in a doorway. She was dressed in a hooded velvet cloak of the most stunning blue. Having been raised a Roman Catholic I sensed a Marian resonance from her. The third night, I had a shamanic dream. This time I was in a bookshop and stretched across its length, was a colossal anaconda. At the head of the snake was a jaguar, the two animals were engaged in a struggle. The next day, after this holy trinity of dreams, kundalini came and life was never the same again.

There is a beautiful word in the Gaelic language, 'cumha' (pronounced coo-ah). In Scottish Gaelic it denotes a lament and is used as a prefix in many of the ancient harp and pipes tunes written to honour the deaths of notable individuals such as clan chieftains. In Irish the meaning is subtler, rather than death, a sense of separation is implied. A Gaelic scholar once described it to me in the following way;

> *'when the immigrants sailed for America leaving behind forever their families and the land of their birth, this was cumha. When the mare is parted from her foal, this is cumha.'*

I found myself, like so many in the western world today, in a state of cumha. Separated from nature and disconnected from source. I anesthetized myself with alcohol and told my ego endless stories. It became clear to me that I was lost. This is the story of my journey home, from cumha, to reconnection.

I had in fact been sensing cumha since childhood. Although I was born in England, my father was Irish and that was our primary cultural influence. We were Irish Roman Catholics in a protestant country and it was quite clear that 'home' was somewhere else. Considering that the English saw me as Irish, and that the Irish saw me as English, I felt myself to be, like the shaman, between worlds from the earliest time.

At the tender age of nine I was introduced to the practice of yoga, a very strange world, which seemed to me, to be completely normal. Every few weeks, with some family friends, I would attend a small yoga retreat centre. Here we did a traditional yoga based on the teaching of an obscure swami. This yoga was quite different from the sanitised commercial versions that predominate today in the West and some of the practices, particularly the yogic purifications, were very advanced. Of these, sutra neti was considered the most important. I was strongly encouraged to do this because I suffered from asthma and chronic rhinitis. Sutra neti involves pushing a rubber catheter up your nostril and through the nasal passage until it emerges at the back of the throat. It is then pulled out with the fingers so that one end is sticking out of the nose and the other the mouth. The nasal passage is then cleared and massaged by pulling the tube back and forth.

To learn this, an ancient yogi took me into a small bathroom. We sat in front of the mirror and I inserted the tube into my nostril. This involved a great deal of sneezing and watering of the eyes until eventually I managed to get the tube to exit at the back of my throat. The next bit is tricky, you have to grip the tube behind the uvula with your first and middle fingers and pull it out of your mouth. You must not pull too much as a length of tube must remain extending out of the nostril and there is a huge gag reflex. I failed miserably at this and eventually the yogi did it for me. I soon became very proficient at sutra neti performing it every day for about three years. Its benefits extend far beyond merely clearing out the nasal passages. Swatramana described the practice of sutra neti in the second chapter of the Hatha Yoga Pradapika where it is called the Neti Karma. He says it is the cleaner of the brain and giver of divine sight.

This yogic experience was further enhanced by my wonderfully exotic and eccentric Irish aunt, Mary Brighid, a woman named after two goddesses. She lived in the USA where she had become heavily involved in siddha yoga. When I was eleven, she returned to visit us and was amazed to find a vegetarian nephew with a knowledge of yoga. She then proceeded to give me dozens of books on yoga, shamanism and general spirituality, which I read avidly. The result was that by the age of twelve, I was quite experienced, both practically and theoretically, in yoga with also a passing knowledge of shamanism and the occult. What are the chances that these opportunities would come to child born into an Irish family, living in an industrial and cultural wasteland, in the 1970's?

In the Bhagavad Gita, Krishna is asked what befalls the yogi that fails to reach completion and Krishna says that the uncompleted yogi will once again be born into circumstances favourable to continuing where they left off on the spiritual path. Looking back at the presence of yoga in my childhood, this indeed would appear to have been the case with me. A yogi once told me that kundalini had come so easily to me in this life as a result of yoga in past incarnations. In a dream of a past life I found myself in a cemetery, the gravestones of my ancestors were all around me. I was guided to a wall covered in family photographs and a voice said, *look, that's you.* In the photograph was a little boy from India. I said, *that's not me* and the voice said emphatically, *it IS you.*

When I was eleven, I fell in love with Irish traditional music, first learning the tin whistle and then progressing to the uilleann pipes. My passion for this music eclipsed all other areas of my life and it was to become my profession in adulthood. Gradually, I forgot my yoga and entered into a sort of spiritual amnesia. I do feel though, that I was given this spiritual education in early life to prepare me for what was to come later on.

In my early twenties my sense of cumha was strong and I went 'home' to Ireland, where I studied for an M.A. in music and met my wife Michèle. It was whilst living in the wildness of the Kerry Mountains, that I received the great dreams often indicative of the shamanic calling. In the first one I found myself standing on an iceberg surrounded by cold clear water. Standing next to me was a polar bear, we dived in and swam together.

This was my first contact with the polar bear as an initiatory animal. All living polar bears are directly descended from ancient Irish bears so the connection makes sense and the polar bear would return to me in the coming years. In the second dream I was standing next to a moonlit pond, an eagle flew down and pulled a serpent out the water. In retrospect, this was clearly about kundalini and higher consciousness, but of course I didn't understand any of this at the time.

Eventually, a culmination of various factors caused us to leave our beloved Ireland, including increasing levels of corruption, rampant materialism and child abuse scandals that we witnessed firsthand. The Ireland of myths, legends and heroes, pipers, harpers and fairies was disappearing as surely as the Firbolg in the wake of the Tuatha De Danaan. With heavy hearts we left Ireland for France.

I had had some moderate success as a musician in Ireland but found myself increasingly out of my comfort zone in France, drinking more and living on past glories and memories. I became increasingly disenchanted with the music I was playing, there was a music deep within me wanting to express itself but it just wasn't possible on the pipes. To this end I acquired an Irish harp, a clairseach and began to reclaim my musical soul. Matching up to its magical reputation in the ancient legends, the clairseach proved to be much more than just a musical instrument. It acted as a spiritual catalyst, reconnecting me to possibilities I had forgotten, I began to play for the divine instead of for my ego.

But it was on the magical island of Bali, that I received clear messages that a spiritual awakening was imminent, although I didn't recognise this at the time. We were staying at an eco-friendly hotel set in tropical forest and one day I asked the barman if there were there many snakes on the island. He assured me in the strongest possible terms that there were absolutely no snakes in Bali. I said that was a shame as I was most interested in snakes. He went off to prepare my drink and I could see he was thinking. When he came back he said, *well, there was one time...* He went on to relate how every morning in the hotel a duck would go missing. Eventually, after a stakeout the mystery was solved, they discovered that a reticulated python was the culprit responsible. Not only is the reticulated python one of the world's largest snakes but this was also one of the largest ever captured. He told me that it could be viewed at the local reptile zoo. As I walked back to my room a small multi-coloured snake whisked across the path in front of me, which made me smile. So much for no snakes in Bali!

As a symbol of kundalini, the snake is intimately connected to yoga and it seems to me that it was no coincidence that this snake appeared on the very day I was to take my first yoga lesson in twenty-five years. The hotel had advertised a class in kundalini yoga and I felt compelled to attend, the word kundalini resonated very strongly with me, even though I had no idea what it was. That afternoon in the class, all of my childhood yoga came flooding back, it was like a homecoming.

The next day we went to see the python, which was indeed most impressive. In another enclosure I was very excited to find a Komodo dragon, as I had always wanted to see such a magnificent animal. The keeper said it was a female and that she was shedding her skin. He went into the enclosure pulled off a piece and gave it to me. I was very happy with this of course but didn't read anything deep into it. Now I realise it was the divine feminine as a dragon, telling me to shed my old skin, to leave behind old ways that were not serving me and become something new. A deeply shamanic communication from the universe, I still have the skin, it is tied to my drum. So, armed with the skin of a dragon and a remembrance of Yoga, I returned to Europe where the unseen forces of the universe would begin to wake me up.

CHAPTER TWO

MY KUNDALINI AWAKENING

When I returned from Bali I straight away began to research yoga and was amazed and a little confused by the vast array of choice available. I initially searched for the type of yoga I did as a child but the yoga centre was gone, the teachers dead and I could find no trace of the swami on the net. Then, it seemed most natural to research kundalini yoga, the 'k word' was still vibrating strongly within in me and I felt guided in this direction. I started off by ordering some kundalini yoga DVD’s. These typically consisted of a warm up set, the main set and a meditation to finish. At the start I was so unfit that I could barely even do the warm up sets but over the following couple of months I did a set everyday and began to enjoy it, particularly the beautiful mantras. This had the effect of strengthening my body and nervous system, which was a good preparation for kundalini to come. Eventually I became drawn much more to the meditation aspect of yoga than the physical asanas. I found myself to be a complete natural at meditation, I seemed to have very little 'monkey mind', and I was able to go to inner silence quickly for long periods of time. After exploring many kinds and methods of meditation I realised that I really needed to concentrate on one practice and I felt strongly guided to an exercise called Sodarshan Chakra Kriya. This is from the school of kundalini Yoga as taught by Yogi Bhajan and is reputed to be the most powerful kriya in all yoga. It is said to raise kundalini, bring psychic powers and bestow many health benefits. This active meditation has a number of components which when combined create an incredibly powerful system.

First you position your eyelids one tenth open and gaze at the tip of your nose. Then you cover your right nostril and breathe in through the left. Once you have breathed in fully you hold your breath and begin to internally chant the mantra, *wahe guru*. At the same time as chanting the mantra you pump your stomach rhythmically, focusing at the navel point. The mantra is chanted sixteen times per breath, which means a total of forty-eight stomach pumps. Following this, you breathe out of the right nostril and start all over again, doing this continually for thirty-one minutes. Gazing at the tip of the nose stimulates the pineal gland, breathing in through the left nostril stimulates the right hemisphere of the brain, pumping the navel point stimulates the kundalini to rise and the mantra stills the mind.

Very soon after starting this meditation I felt energy rise up all around my pelvis, it was very sexual, very pleasant but I was certainly rather frightened. It did confirm to me though that this legendary kundalini energy was a reality and it gave me the encouragement needed to carry on. For the next few months absolutely nothing happened during my meditations but I continued, it just seemed like the right thing to do and I really had no expectations. Of course, once you start a regular meditation practice, it might seem like nothing is happening but in fact major changes may be taking place on many levels. During this time, something I now recognise as the divine at work happened. I was sitting in the hairdressers, when suddenly the thought came to me, that we should sell our nice big house, and move to the country and try to live in a far more natural way. I went back to the café where Michèle was waiting and ran the idea by her. She loved it immediately and we straightaway set about putting the plan in motion.

After some months of searching we still hadn't found the perfect place. I had seen one property, which seemed right but it was out of our price range. Despite this, we did enquire, but found it had been sold. Sometime later we were in an estate agents and saw the property again for sale. It turned out the sale had fallen through and due to the economic crisis it was now available, at a considerably reduced price. We went to visit the house and fell in love, not with the house but with the land. Twenty-four acres of prairie, woods, drystone walls and a one kilometre drive up an un-tarmacked walking path to get there. It was perfect for our cats and perfect for us, as we wanted to lead a more ecological self-sufficient lifestyle. The house however was a complete wreck, built in 1789 it was in need of total renovation, the roof leaked, the windows and doors didn't close, you had to go outside to go upstairs, water came in but didn't go out and to top it off, the man we bought the house from had been keeping his goats in it and the smell was appalling! That would not have been a problem if we had had money for repairs but we didn’t, we’d used all we had to get the property and our old house just wasn't selling. Despite this, we moved into these terrible conditions both physical and financial, as it just seemed like the right thing to do. We endured for two years before the other house sold and despite the fact that in winter it snowed inside the house and the temperature in the bedroom was only two degrees, the sight of owls, hares and herds of deer in the fields made up for it all.

I feel certain that through being stripped of physical comfort and financial security whilst at the same time being in a wild natural environment, that perfect conditions were being created for my kundalini to awaken. I spent more and more time going into the forest to meditate. I soon began to feel energy bubbling strongly up my spine from the area of the sacrum. As soon as I sat down to meditate it would rise up to between my shoulder blades and stop. I began to get some back pain, which made meditation difficult but I was motivated to continue. I have to say that I found this interesting but not spiritual. It was interesting in that it further confirmed to me that the kundalini was actually real, but it was in no way a spiritual feeling, physically it felt quite neutral, neither pleasant nor unpleasant. I was very happy to be having this experience but honestly did not expect anything more, that would be the preserve of the great saints and sages, a category which I didn't and still don't fall into! After a couple of weeks of this I had the trinity of dreams described at the start of the narrative, of Isis, the goddess in blue and the anaconda and the jaguar. This last dream was particularly important. I knew that snake dreams often accompanied kundalini awakening and initially I simply regarded the anaconda as kundalini, which of course at one level it was. I didn't understand the jaguar at all. It wasn't until years later when I went to South America, to drink the shamanic entheogen ayahuasca, that I discovered the Peruvian trinity of Serpent (kundalini), Feline (you in this reality), and Condor (higher consciousness). Then, I understood the jaguar as my ego-self, fighting the kundalini about to rise. However, this was not only a dream of kundalini awakening, it was at the same time a shamanic initiation. The anaconda and the jaguar are both avatars of ayahuasca, which is in fact a kundalini plant. From the very first, the shamanic animal and plant spirits were calling me.

The next morning after these three dreams I sat down to meditate and as usual, energy bubbled up my spine to between my shoulder blades but then something happened, the energy changed completely in character. It was no longer thick and bubbly, it became very sharp and focused and whipped suddenly in a snake-like motion up my left shoulder blade, up the back of my neck and into my brainstem. The feeling of the energy is very difficult to describe. The words electric, sensual, fiery, all come to mind but fail to convey, even a combination of all of them does not come close. It felt like my brainstem had been injected with some strange living liquid intent on entering my brain. I have to say I got a bit scared at this point, in fact my heart was beating like mad as I had read many of the scare stories of people going mad or being hospitalised or incapacitated as a result of kundalini awakening. Now the thing is, I wasn't actually really afraid of any of these phenomena, it was just that it would be very inconvenient. I was just about to go on tour and so a lot of people were depending on me. In retrospect what seems really crazy is that the great goddess of creation was rising up within me, giving that most rare and exquisite of blessings and that my western mind was saying, *actually Goddess, this is really not a good time, things to do, people to see, maybe catch you later, you know how it is!* Anyway, I prayed for it to go back down and eventually it receded. After some time I gathered myself together and attempted to go about my day, but all day I could feel kundalini still subtly residing at my brainstem.

That evening I was compelled to sit down again in meditation. This time I had absolutely no control whatsoever. The kundalini whipped straight into my brainstem and up into my brain, which is undoubtedly the most strange and shocking sensation I have ever experienced. From this point on I could see the kundalini inside me as a point of light, like a mini comet. I became aware at this stage also that it was intelligent and had an agenda. I sensed strongly it was searching for something, that 'something' being the crown chakra where Her consort was waiting. This mini comet proceeded to spiral round and round my brain finding the pineal and pituitary glands, the glands physically associated with the third eye and crown chakras. Energy began spiralling over my forehead and then on the top of my head. Round and round it spiralled, inwards, inwards, until it reached the fontanel. At this point the kundalini exited the fontanel (I could feel this distinctly), and headed for the crown chakra, which is actually located above the head. When the awakened goddess within me reached the crown she unified with her god, the great still consciousness of the Universe. As the union occurred, the energy of unification fountained down upon me as light. At this point a round patch of heat about the size of a coin formed at my fontanel. This became very hot indeed, not painful, but far hotter than any part of the human body is supposed to get. This patch of heat then expanded outwards and downwards to cover my whole head like a helmet, then from there, big drops of light energy poured down my body, and it was over. I think I was perhaps in a state of shock and really not sure about what had happened. I understood that something truly extraordinary had occurred but as far as I could tell I was neither insane nor enlightened, did this mean it wasn't kundalini awakening? I was later to realise that kundalini awakening is not the end but really just the start. I went outside, sat on the steps and thought about how they certainly don't teach you about this in school!

Life went on but the kundalini energy remained with me, it was particularly noticeable in the forehead/third eye region. I continued with various yoga exercises and meditations, as I didn't want it to go away. I didn't realise that this was to be a permanent condition. I didn't understand that the unified energies of Shakti and Shiva were now beginning the long process of transforming every aspect of my being, a process that continues to this day.

Over the ensuing months I began occasionally to experience some rather odd internal phenomena. The first was explosions of light in my head. It was like someone was letting off a firecracker in the centre of my brain. This would occur when I was relaxed and lying down but not asleep. It wasn't at all painful and actually rather fun. Another phenomenon was hearing my name called, out of nowhere a clear female voice would softly say, *Brendan*. One day, I was lying on my bed and right from the centre of my head an owl hooted very loudly. Somehow I knew that this was going to happen again and it did, straight away. I told an Indian friend about this and he got quite excited. He informed me that that night, there had been a special moon, sacred to the Goddess Lakshmi. On this night it is said that whoever Lakshmi visits will receive financial blessings, he said our money problems would soon be over. Indeed, the next day our house was sold. Lakshmi is nearly always depicted with an owl.

Around this time I also had occasional out of body experiences. I'm no expert in astral projection, it is not something I have pursued but it still happens occasionally, usually to give me some kind of teaching or information. The first time it happened was actually before kundalini came. I was lying in bed and I literally fell out of my body and began floating up to the ceiling. I remember seeing Michèle below me, and calling out to her but of course I couldn't make any noise. I continued to float up through the ceiling and got stuck in the attic before being drawn back down into my body. Another time I woke and I could see a moon some distance from me, as I focused on this, very loud machine type noises began, like cogs grinding against each other. I knew I was about to leave my body and when I did I decided to fly. I flew high over our village before getting confused and being pulled back into my body once again. These experiences were quite fun but one OBE was more serious. I was pulled out of my body and taken high into the sky. There, I encountered a sort of matrix/web of blue light. I could press against it and it would move but I couldn't pass through it and I was brought back down. When I came back I entered a sort of dream state, I could see a being made of orange light sitting at the foot of the bed, I sensed strongly that it was a tiger. On the chair next to my bed I could see a huge beetle like a stag beetle or a scarab. The meaning of the scarab in ancient Egypt was, *he who is to become.*

As well as these phenomena, my dream life took on a whole new character and became almost more real to me at times than waking life. Early kundalini dreams were very intense.

There is a shimmering mist; Michèle and I are naked, floating over a moonlit pond. Rising out of the pond is a huge spine, it is risen up like a snake. I am scared of it. It bends down, penetrates my root chakra and we are lost in ecstasy.

Another time I looked out of a window onto a misty lawn. I could see a group of naked dancers forming the shape of a chakra. A woman came forward from the rest and a voice said, *this is the Goddess of the Moon*. She looked straight at me.

CHAPTER THREE

KUNDALINI AND SHAMANISM

It is in India that the phenomena of kundalini awakening has been observed, preserved and most clearly elucidated. It is therefore not surprising that India should produce one of the most eloquent authors on the subject, Gopi Krishna. His simple definitions of kundalini remain the best,

> *'Kundalini is the super-intelligent Energy behind consciousness.' 1*
>
> *'...there are two aspects of the Power: First the individual aspect where She can be said to be lying dormant at the base of the spine, and second Her cosmic aspect, which is beyond our understanding.' 2*

Looking first at this cosmic aspect, it is perhaps not too huge a leap, for even the most Cartesian mind, to consider that there may be a primal creative energetic force behind all the phenomena of the known universe, as yet unidentified by western science. The spiritual sciences of India long ago established the reality of this force and named it Shakti. Shakti is a Sanskrit word that can be translated as meaning power or energy. It is derived from the verb root 'shak', which means 'to be able', 'to do', 'to act'. It was also recognised that this force was feminine in nature, a creative mother energy. It is in this way that it presents itself to the aspirant, hence my dreams of Isis and the goddess in blue. In Hinduism, Shakti is personified as a goddess of the same name and the awakened kundalini in the individual becomes known as Shakti. It is considered that the primal goddess of creation is flowing in the person. This concept of a primal feminine creative power is expressed in the kundalini yoga, Adi Shakti mantra.

> *Adi Shakti, Adi Shakti, Adi Shakti, Namo, Namo*
> *Sarab a Shakti, Sarab a Shakti, Sarab a Shakti, Namo, Namo*
> *Prithum Bhagvatee, Prithum Bhagvatee, Prithum Bhagvatee, Namo Namo*
> *Kundalini Mata Shakti, Mata Shakti, Namo, Namo*
> *(Primal She-Power, Salutations to Thee!*
> *All-Encompassing She-Power, Salutations to Thee!*
> *That through which Divine Creates, Salutations to Thee!*
> *Creative Power of the Kundalini, Mother of all Mother Power, Salutations!)*

This is the cosmic aspect of kundalini, which as Gopi Krishna says, is beyond our understanding. This cosmic feminine energetic force resides at the base of every human spine as latent spiritual potential, curled three and a half times like a spring or a serpent ready to strike. On the biological level Gopi Krishna has this to say of kundalini awakening,

> *'...energy goes from the body to the brain like a radiant stream of light...The enlightened person has these two characteristics: a new area in the brain springs to activity, and a new form of energy rises through the spinal cord into the brain.'3*

Kundalini moves through the spiritual nervous system which overlays and sometimes coincides with our biological nervous system. The spiritual nervous system consists of the chakras (energy wheels) and nadis (energy channels or rivers). Of the nadis the most important is the sushumna, which means 'auspicious'. The sushumna is the principle spiritual nerve in the body and runs along the spinal column from the root chakra (mooladhara), located at the perineum, to the third eye (ajna chakra), in the centre of the forehead just above the eyes. In fact, from there, it extends out and upwards into the cosmos. This is what the ancient Egyptians were depicting with the cobra coming out of the pharaoh's forehead. Either side of sushumna are the two other principle nadis, ida and pingala. Ida is the moon channel and pingala is the sun channel. It is necessary for these two nadis to come into complimentary balance for the kundalini to rise up the sushumna.

The mechanics of an awakening are as follows. The kundalini energy, at the base of the spine, moves up through the sushumna, through the chakras located on the spine, into the brainstem and then the brain. It then moves through certain nadis in the brain going through the pineal and pituitary glands until it is perceived as exiting the head at the area known as the fontanel. It is surely no coincidence that kundalini is felt rising in the area called the sacrum (sacred) and exits, 'fountaining' at the fontanel. It is clear to me that these names were given with full knowledge of the kundalini process. Upon exiting the fontanel a union of energy occurs, a little way above the head. This is a unification of female and male polarities, usually termed Shakti and Shiva. The energy then returns back down into the individual, continuing a process of transformation lasting years or lifetimes. What I have described here is an ideal version, in reality there are an infinite amount of variables and each person will have a slightly different experience.

There are many ways that kundalini is felt in the body, it is certainly both a biological and spiritual energy. On the biological level the sensation of it is as tangible as any other physical sensation one might have. It is obvious to the person within whom the energy is moving that it is working directly upon the physical body, that at one level an evolutionary upgrade is being received. The energetic sensations are felt initially most strongly at the base of the spine in the area known as the sacrum. The energy can be discerned entering the sushumna from this point. It may be felt as a very fine sharp energy, or as heat or cold, or as large bubbles. It may move slowly or extremely fast. Basically there is no restriction on how it may manifest, the only prerequisite for defining kundalini is that there must be energy moving within the spinal column. This is not the only place it will be but it has to be there. It may feel like insects crawling on the skin, it may feel like being stung. The left side of the body and face may go numb as if being anesthetised at the dentist. It may be felt at all chakra points, pulsing at the root or wrapping like a snake around the throat. It may be felt in arms and hands, legs in feet. Even the genital area may become ecstatic. It may rise up the front of the body as well as the back. It may be felt deep within the stomach, in the teeth, the eyes and nose. It may be as specific as having an intensely blissful nose tip, or it may be everywhere at once.

For me, the physical presence of kundalini is always immediate, if I simply turn my attention inward. However it may come at any time during everyday activity. I may find myself having a conversation but at the same time have ecstatic energy moving in my crown chakra and third eye. Divine sounds may be heard; I have woken in the night to hear thousands of crickets around me, the sound of water rushing through me, or the crystalline tinkling of tiny bells. In the right ear one may perceive the sound of kundalini in the sushumna. As kundalini begins to awaken our spiritual heart we may see fireflies, fire and smoke within us, we may see the full moon and the rising of the internal sun.

Other physical manifestations are known as kriyas. In yoga a kriya is a set of movements, which combine towards a certain end. Kundalini yoga uses kriyas to attempt the raising of kundalini. The fact however, is that yoga is the gift of kundalini and not the other way round. I have found that many of the sitting and breathing exercises found in kundalini yoga happen spontaneously to the kundalini-awakened person in meditation. Arching of the spine, bending forward, twisting from side to side, the tongue going back in the mouth, bouncing up and down, strange vocalisations. These movements were clearly observed in kundalini-awakened people and then incorporated into yoga in the hope that imitation would bring about the same results.

As the awakened kundalini moves through every cell in the body, more and more of the spiritual nervous system becomes enlivened. Traumas from this and past lives accrue in this spiritual nervous system as blockages and as the kundalini progresses, it clears these blockages and traumas. In this way kundalini clears what we might think of as certain aspects of karma. Although this spiritual nervous system remains largely undetected and ignored by western science it is very real to the awakened person.

Kundalini may bring spectacular visions and experiences in order to shake the person to the very core of their beliefs about the nature of existence. Although most phenomena are experienced internally, sometimes visions may be given, to be seen with open eyes, in ordinary reality. Visions of this nature are the exception rather than the rule and although we crave more, we only need to see the Divine in this form once, after this we must learn to see the Divine in everything. Because we are rooted in the concept that what we see with open eyes is the true reality, visions that manifest here serve to reaffirm the truth of our experience and from there we may move on to inner visions with less questioning of their validity.

After a time the manifestations and experience become more subtle, as more and more of what the person is not, is stripped away and more and more of the true self begins to shine through, expressing out into daily life and those around them. Indeed, those close to the awakened one may certainly be effected by the process as they are drawn into the karmic vortex that kundalini initiates. Kundalini puts a person onto a karmic fast track, seeking in one lifetime to burn through as much karma as possible. This means that whatever residual negative karma there is will come but on the plus side, all the positive karma will come too. It should be understood that the search for truth and the process of spiritual awakening is not a selfish pursuit. In fact that desire to know the Self is the most selfless pursuit we can undertake because changing our own consciousness may catalyse the process in others and this is really the only way we can effect positive change in the world.

The Katha Upanishad says,

> *'Those who see themselves in all and all in them help others through spiritual Osmosis to realise the Self in themselves.'*

Judee Sill is a largely forgotten singer/songwriter from the nineteen seventies. She was a musical genius with a deeply spiritual aspect to her work. She made some live recordings for the seminal British music programme, The Old Grey Whistle Test. Among them, her incredibly beautiful song, 'The Kiss'. In her introduction she says, this song is about the union of opposites that we all have and the kiss is a symbol of that union. This is a perfect description of kundalini awakening and makes me think that perhaps she knew more than she was telling. Her lyrics describe beautifully the subtle sense of divine presence that tends to pervade the kundalini awakening process, *holy breath, touching me like a wind song.*

The principle catalyst in kundalini awakening is the soul's wish to return to Oneness. There are three main ways in which kundalini awakening may occur. It may come from self-initiation through intense spiritual desire (bhakti), it may be transmitted from guru to disciple (shaktipat) or it may be induced through spiritual austerities. Of the latter, yoga, for thousands of years has been the tried and tested method for safely raising the kundalini energy. Details of the various yogic methods for awakening kundalini can be found in the Kundalini Yoga Upanishad and the Hatha Yoga Pradapika. Yoga is the antidote to cumha, for me, yoga is the science of experiential remembrance of who we are.

The boundaries between yoga and shamanism are certainly quite blurred in places but ultimately their goals are different. Just as Gopi Krishna is the definitive voice on kundalini, the same came be said of Mercia Eliade on shamanism. Here he eloquently expresses the essential difference between the two.

'But let us emphasise... the structural difference that distinguishes classic yoga from shamanism. Although the latter is not without certain techniques of concentration its final goal is always ecstasy and the souls ecstatic journey through the various cosmic regions, whereas yoga pursues enstsasis, final concentration of the spirit and 'escape' from the cosmos.' 4

Kundalini awakening and shamanic awakening should not be confused as necessarily the same thing. Kundalini awakening is the process of enlightenment, its function is to bring the person home into self-realisation. Not all kundalini-awakened people will be shamans. Shamanic awakening on the other hand is not primarily about enlightenment but about creating an individual that can be an intermediary between here and the spirit worlds, what Eliade calls, a technician of the sacred. Yogis have studied and written about kundalini awakening with scientific precision but the same cannot be said of shamanic awakening which is an equally mysterious process.

In a shamanic spiritual awakening it is not the individual but the shamanic spirits that are the principle catalyst. The shamanic spirits may be considered as disincarnate consciousnesses in the form of animals, plants, ancestors, and shamans. Broadly speaking there are three main ways that a person may become a shaman. Firstly, it may be in the family and they continue the tradition, sometimes the helper spirits pass from one family member to another. Secondly, an individual may simply feel a strong calling and seek out a teacher. Thirdly, the person may undergo a shamanic spiritual awakening having been 'chosen' by the spirits. Even in traditional societies there may be an element of fear surrounding this possibility, there is a sense of choice being taken away, of accepting a destiny not desired. Traditionally the person must accept the calling, non-acceptance may lead to an unhappy life or even death. In some traditions it is considered that shamans are born not made, that even though the calling may not manifest until adulthood, a spirit has bonded with them from birth. Sometimes the shaman is likened to a cuckoo, raised in the same nest as its siblings but not the same. As with kundalini awakening, the process itself may be difficult and confusing, all the more so for a western person in a culture with absolutely no reference point for this class of phenomena.

During visions, dreams and ecstasies, the shamanic spirits teach and alter the shaman through attacks and dismemberments and inserting objects like crystals into the shamans' spiritual body. The shamanic sickness is a particularly mysterious characteristic of this kind of awakening. As a child, Black Elk, the Oglala Sioux medicine man was struck down with a mysterious illness for a number of days during which he remained in a comatose state completely unresponsive to any treatment. It is during this time that the spirits come and he receives his great vision and after this he becomes a healer. This is a classic example of shamanic sickness. There is currently a trend to view certain forms of mental illness as shamanic sicknesses and while there is little doubt that some people undergoing the phenomena of shamanic spiritual awakening have been diagnosed as mentally ill, not all mentally ill people are misdiagnosed shamans.

Usually, initiation by spirits is backed up by training from a human elder shaman. In the modern context it should be noted that you can't buy the former and without this the latter is irrelevant. In the west, training from an elder shaman from an ancient lineage is an unrealistic expectation and in any case it is the non-human initiatory aspect that is of primary importance.

> *'...sicknesses, dreams and ecstasies in themselves constitute an initiation; that is, they transform the profane, pre-choice individual into a technician of the sacred.' 5*

Shamanism and yoga may certainly combine harmoniously as one. That shamanic yogas may have existed is supported by Pantajali in his famous Yoga Sutras where he refers to certain medicinal plants (ausadhi) that in equal measure with samadhi, can give the yogin miraculous powers. As Eliade points out,

> *'...the protohistorical origins of classic yoga in no sense exclude the existence of intermediate forms of shamanic yoga directed to obtaining particular ecstatic experiences.' 6*

The word 'shaman' is said to come from the Tunguskan word saman, which may be translated as 'one who knows'. After encountering Siberian shamans western explorers and anthropologists began to apply the term to all the traditional healers/spirit workers they encountered in other parts of the world. So the word shamanism was invented and entered the English language to describe any form of indigenous healing practice, despite the fact that they are incredibly diverse in nature. In this sense it is best really to talk of 'shamanisms' rather than shamanism but that said, irrespective of culture or geographical location, the shamanisms of the world exhibit far more similarities to each other than differences.

The shamanisms of the far north, of the Inuit, the Sami and Siberia all display knowledge of kundalini in various ways. From Siberia, where it is said that all shamanism originated, comes the oldest wooden statue in the world, the Shigir Idol. It was preserved in a peat bog and is estimated at 9,500 years old. It can be viewed in the Yekaterinburg History Museum. Professor Mikhail Zhilin, leading researcher of the Russian Academy of Sciences' Institute of Archaeology said,

'We study the idol with a feeling of awe. This is a masterpiece, carrying gigantic emotional value and force. It is a unique sculpture, there is nothing else in the world like this. It is very alive and very complicated at the same time. The ornament is covered with encrypted information. People were passing on knowledge with the help of the idol.' 7

Currently the idol stands 2.8 meters tall but originally was more likely 5.3 meters. Depicted on it are seven faces distributed on both front and back. Six of these faces are one dimensional, the seventh one on the top of the idol being three-dimensional. The faces on the idol are staggered up its length and linked by snaking zigzag patterns and markings very similar to those found on the handles of Siberian drums representing the vertebrae of the spirit figure, the ongon. It is very clear to me that this idol is depicting the six chakras on the spine, the zigzag pattern representing the snake-like movement of kundalini. The seventh face, being the only fully formed three-dimensional one, can be seen as the crown chakra.

Professor Zhilin observed that the people that created the idol,

'...lived in perfect harmony with the world, had advanced intellectual development, and a complicated spiritual world.' 8

Miraculously, they have left us a clear depiction of knowledge of the spiritual awakening process from the Mesolithic Stone Age.

In Inuit shamanism the master shaman obtains the angacok for the apprentice.

> *'Then the master obtains the angakoq...the disciples 'lighting' or 'enlightenment', for the angakoq consists of a mysterious light which the shaman suddenly feels in his body, inside his head, within the brain, an inexplicable searchlight, a luminous fire...'* 9

The fact that the shaman 'obtains' this luminous fire for the initiate does seem strikingly similar to the process of shaktipat in India.

The designs on the drums of the Sami people provide some of the most valuable insights into shamanic cosmology. Hundreds of these drums were burnt by missionaries along with their owners the Sami shaman, the noaide. On a detailed drawing fortunately preserved of one of the lost drums, there is a clear depiction of kundalini. The serpent passes through the three shamanic worlds, spiralling around a central line representing the spine. At either end of the serpent are the sun and the moon representing ida and pingala nadis and the unification of male and female energies.

In North America a Navaho sand painting to a blessing chant from New Mexico (1950) shows clearly a union of opposites and energy ascending a central column with different levels. This represents a spiritual ascent along what the Navaho call the Pollen Path. Campbell notes that,

> *'The parallelism of the tantric visionary ascent of the sushumna and the ritually controlled transit of the Navaho Pollen Path is not so simple to explain.' 10*

And that,

> *'The conformity of this particular sand painting to the sense and symbolised experiences of the yogic sushumna is certainly astonishing...' 11*

In Africa, the San on the Kalahari, call kundalini n/um, it rises up their spines like a rope connecting them to Heaven. The Zulu call kundalini, umbalini, the two words are strikingly similar. The indigenous peoples of Australia have the Rainbow Serpent.

In South America, we see the trinity of serpent, feline and condor representing the kundalini awakening process. The Q'ero, shaman-mystics of the Andes, speak of the siki, located at the base of the spine from where there is,

> *'...a specific kundalini-like movement of energy, visualised as a serpent of light, that can be unleashed from the siki...' 12*

In the Amazon, the entheogen Ayahuasca, a snake-like vine, ascends a tree-spine as the feminine principle, earth energy seeking the sun. The San Pedro cactus, a phallic masculine entheogen compliments this union of polarities.

So it can be seen, from this by no means comprehensive list of examples, that kundalini is a fundamental principle underlying various shamanisms of the world and also the source and goal of the spiritual science of yoga. Both kundalini awakening and shamanic awakening bring the individual into awareness of the illusory nature of reality. If we take the analogy of water as pure consciousness, then what we experience here is snow. Here, consciousness is condensed, you can shape and mold snow in ways that you can't with water in its pure state. It is this way so that we are not overwhelmed. Both yogi and shaman learn to navigate the waters of consciousness, they learn to swim where others might drown. Until, through our yearning to return home we awaken the goddess within, we remain as children, playing in the snow.

CHAPTER FOUR

SNAKES AND THE WEB OF ONENESS

Surrender to the song, surrender to the way of God, surrender to Kundalini.
Mantra received in a dream.

With me, there have been two main avatars of kundalini Shakti, the snake and the spider. Broadly speaking, they represent the two aspects of the power described by Gopi Krishna. The snake may be seen as the coiled aspect at the base of the individual's spine, the spider as the cosmic aspect beyond our understanding.

Kundalini Shakti is often represented as a snake. One of the reasons for this is that she chooses to manifest in this form to the aspirant in dreams and visions. People in kundalini awakening often have recurring snake dreams. This is partly because as the kundalini moves up the tube of the sushumna and in and out of the valves leading to the chakras, the mind asks itself, *what could possibly fit in this space and move in this way?* More often than not, the mind comes up with a snake.

There are many different kinds of snakes in my dreams from tiny venomous ones to frighteningly large constrictors. The poisonous snakes want to bite me, their poison is an agent of death and therefore transformation. The huge constrictors serve to remind me of the coils of Maya, which enfold us in ignorance of our true nature. I don't see these snakes as power animals or spirits in the shamanic sense but as pure manifestations of Shakti Kundalini, the mind's interpretation of the spiritual processes occurring.

The reticulated python I first saw in Bali has come many times. Initially She revealed the feminine aspect of Herself.

I see a HUGE snake on a wall. It's a reticulated python. It's really beautiful with gorgeous skin patterning in many different colours. The snake changes into a woman, she stands up and jumps off the wall. We link arms and we walk and talk, she says, 'I want to be with you forever'.

In the following dream She reveals Herself as that which binds us here.

I see a beautiful lake filled to the brim with still cold water. A reticulated python sits on my lap and nuzzles my face.

This dream shows pure consciousness as the lake with kundalini Shakti as the python saying, *look at me, I am the illusion keeping you from this.*

In this dream She reveals definitively Her aspect as creator of the illusion.

I see a reticulated python, it's in a booth at a zoo. It has huge teeth and rubs its head all over me like a cat, she talks to me and tells me her name, her name is Maya.

Although her name is Maya and in this aspect she functions as concealer of truth, in her manifestation as the cobra and other venomous varieties of snake, she becomes the revealer, if you will let her bite you. Initially of course I was afraid.

I'm standing in a street, with myself, as a young boy. We are looking in a shop window, which is full of snakes. A man appears and picks up a King Cobra. He opens the hood and presses the snake's head against the window. The cobra's fangs are huge but I tell the boy not to be afraid.

Over time I began to allow these snakes to bite me. In this dream I am being asked to make myself a home, for kundalini Shakti.

I'm given a small wooden box. Inside it is a small red and white striped snake. A voice says, 'Can you make a box for this?' The snake opens its mouth to a vast proportion and bites my hand.

Eventually I learned to relax into the process and love the snakes that were biting me.

I dream I'm on a bed with my dad. A black mamba is chewing my hand. I stroke its head. I see a huge cobra with green and white stripes by the door.

This dream shows the divine masculine as my father, and the mamba as divine feminine, the bed symbolising the unification. The cobra with its two colours represents the witness of this unification at the doorway to self-realisation.

The shamanic aspect of kundalini presents itself most often as an anaconda. In these two dreams I think at first that the anaconda is dead or sleeping but in fact it is only dormant and reveals itself as a great and terrifying force awakening within me.

I'm walking along our lane. I see a snake, a small patterned anaconda. I think it's dead, I prod it with a stick, it comes alive, stretches out, forming a bridge across the path, now it is huge. My cats are with me, I'm afraid they will be eaten. A small Native-American child appears, she tells me not to worry.

In the second dream I saw an anaconda of monumental proportions lying in heaped coils in a field. I was with a friend and we walked between the coils thinking that the snake was dead. Then suddenly it reared up above us, I screamed to my friend but then the snake transformed into a human and vanished into thin air.

Sometimes Michèle is in the snake dreams, reminding me that I am not taking this journey alone, that others are drawn in. In one dream Michèle and I walked in a river in a forest. In the river were many rocks and lying on the rocks were cobras, we just kept on walking through the water. Before going to take ayahuasca a snake dream delivered a wonderful and amazing divine communication. I found myself standing in a small clearing in the forest. Michèle was sitting in a car repeating over and over, like a mantra, the number twenty-six. As she chanted, a green snake with a black stripe down its back, passed by my feet through the grass. Subsequent research revealed that the numerical value of the name of God in Hebrew, formed of the Hebraic letters yod, he, waw and he,

YHWH, is 10+5+6+5, which adds up to twenty six. This name of four letters giving twenty-six is found in the fourth chapter of Genesis with its twenty six verses, beginning with Adam and ending by the name of God. By using as a correspondence table, A=1, B=2, ..., Z=26, we find that the name of the divine in English, GOD, gives also twenty-six. Michèle had been chanting the numerical name of god as the kundalini serpent slithered by.

The spider occurs in many cultures as a feminine creative principle. It has eight legs, the number eight turned on its side becomes the symbol for infinity. The Vedas compare God and the physical universe we experience to a spider and a spider's web. The spider's web comes out of the spider and the spider resides within the web itself. Similarly our physical universe has been created out of the Oneness and the Oneness pervades all things in the universe. The Oneness is both the container of the universe as well as what is contained inside it.

The Upanishads say, *Brahman is like a spider catching everything in its net but itself moving freely through it untouched.* We remain ensnared until we realise the web is entirely of our own making. In the same way that our consciousness interprets the energy moving within us as a snake, the best the mind can come up with in attempting to process something far beyond its capability is to present us with a spider.

One of the first spider dreams I remember is one where I was in the cellar of an old castle. There was a spiral staircase going up but to get there we had to pass under huge spider webs containing giant black spindly spiders. I was not happy about this but Michèle went ahead and I followed. In another dream we returned to the same cellar and it was full of giant spider egg sacs. These dreams were showing me that in order to ascend the spiral of consciousness I had to pass through the webs of illusion and that these webs are created and hatched deep in the cellars of the subconscious.

Sometimes, as with the snakes, the spiders wanted to bite me, reflective of their transformative aspect as bringers of death. In my dreams I have been bitten by a black widow spider, a symbol of the goddess, in her dark aspect. I was also bitten on the inner thigh by a baby bird-eating spider. It is good to be bitten by the spiders in dreams; it is a surrendering to the process, an allowing of the venom to destroy the illusion of which the spider is the original creator.

Twice I have woken to the presence of spirit spiders in my bed. The first time I awoke to find a huge spider walking up and down on my stomach, its abdomen changing constantly to different chakra colours. On the second occasion I saw a brown spirit tarantula running into the bed and under the covers. I just went back to sleep, if it had been a real one I would have been out of the bed in a shot!

At other times I find that I am shown something in a dream and then I notice the presence of a spider there also. I sense this is a way of telling me, *pay attention, this is important.*

I find myself standing on some steps. There are people looking at a swarm of bees. The bees are huge. I see there is a tarantula standing on the steps next to me.

A swarm of bees is a metaphor for the Oneness and the illusion. Bees may appear separate but a hive is in fact one organism. The spider on the steps is saying,

I am THAT.

I'm on a bus journey. When it's time to get off I can't, because I find I have too much rubbish. Amongst other things I have a draw full of old computer floppy disks. Then I see a huge tarantula crawl up the wall and onto the ceiling, it is very beautiful, black with yellow stripes.

This dream was telling me I can't get off at the final destination until I have rid myself of outmoded ways of being (the floppy disks). The spider as the Oneness will bring me to the final destination of itself.

Most profoundly the spider has brought messages of the eternal self, that which is present in, yet beyond all states of consciousness and phenomena. In one dream I saw a caterpillar transforming into a spider. Normally the caterpillar transforms into a butterfly, but the butterfly is not the final transformation, the spider is. In another dream Michèle gave me a sword in a scabbard. I carefully pulled out the sword to reveal a large spider in the scabbard. The sword my weapon to cut through illusion is also kundalini which when unsheathed reveals the presence of the spider all along.

In a dream I see my mother, she shows me two huge orb-weaver spiders on either side of the room. I realise I'm in the living room of my childhood home and the room is filled with a massive spider's web, it is crystalline, it looks like it's made of light. My sister walks across the room to my mother and I see that the web is attached to her and moves with her. From this I understand that through the web, we are all connected to each other and the Mother. In the web I see a small spider, it is completely transparent, made of silvery light, very beautiful. Then a grasshopper crawls out of the web. I say, *that's not the spider* and a voice says, *it IS*. It washes contentedly then returns to the web, wraps itself in silk and becomes a pupa. Everything that emanates from the web is the One, all is the spider, the Oneness. Between lives we emerge from the web of illusion content in our remembrance, until our unfilled desires draw us back and we once more bind ourselves in the web of illusion and forgetting.

In meditation I saw a pair of hands. They made a movement and a black spider appeared in a palm. In Kashmir Shaivism the illusion is likened to a kind of magic trick, this was like seeing the hands of the conjuror. The spider walked around shapeshifting, again showing itself as everything in many forms. Then I saw a matchbox, it opened and now the spider was inside. Then I felt it dancing on my crown chakra, the spider both within the container and containing everything. Then a sri-yantra appeared, that perfect depiction of microcosm and macrocosm, I heard many people singing *om namah shivaye*, I began to sing.

In a powerful dream, Michèle and I walk into an open-air cinema. On the big screen an Indian woman is singing mantras and everyone begins to sing along. Above me, from the sky, a giant butterfly descends over my crown chakra. On top of the butterfly, like the turiya state in the Om symbol sits a green spider. A man comes and places a hawk on Michèle's arm and then on mine and another spider walks repeatedly up and down in front of us. Two huge beautiful snakes come towards us very fast. As they are moving they are shedding their skins to reveal gorgeous patterns underneath. A female voice sings, *place every action in the heart, place every action in the heart.*

CHAPTER FIVE

THE SPIRITS OF THE SOUL

Interspersing these repetitive snake and spider dreams the power animals began to come. They are the essential companions of the shaman and one of the ways in which shamanism differs from all other spiritual modalities. As non-human intelligences with their own individual existence and purpose, they are, ultimately, like the cosmic aspect of kundalini beyond the comprehension and rationalisation of the human mind. Eliade says that the shamans' principle animal is in a manner his double, his alter ego, his soul in animal form. I have come to view them as aspects of the Oneness, the One Soul in myriad animal forms. I like to call them the Spirits of the Soul.

For me there have been four main categories of power animal. The first is the totem or principle animal. This is your guardian, is always with you and may remain with you for life. The second kind is the journey animal. This is an animal that comes for a certain period of time to help you with a specific task or particular aspect of your life journey. The third is the messenger animal. As its name suggests it comes to give a specific message, sometimes a warning. The fourth kind is the shadow animal. This animal represents your fears, addictions or negative behaviour patterns. It is usually an animal that scares you. By facing up to this animal, by overcoming what it represents to you in life, it may become your ally.

These animals may come in dreams, visions, shamanic journeys and sometimes also in real life. In real life, for it to be a spirit animal it will usually tend to be behaving in an unusual manner or in an unusual place to emphasise that this is a spirit communication. The first of these to come was the barn owl. One morning I got up and went into the kitchen and made myself some coffee as usual. I intended to sit in the living room on the window seat and enjoy the view with my coffee. As soon as I opened the door something huge flew over my head and I backed out in a panic. Once I had composed myself I slowly opened the door again, and there sitting on the table was a barn owl. I took a few seconds to enjoy the wonder of the moment, before opening the window and leaving the room, so it could find its way out in peace. Years later I had another encounter when a barn owl landed in our field, in broad daylight. I hear many owls here in our woods at night, but seldom a barn owl, they are rare in these parts, and to observe one during the day is unusual to say the least. I was able to watch it for some time before it left for the woods.

The next morning the fields and woods were shrouded in deep mist, there was a beautiful magical quality in the air, so I decided to take my dog, Dougal, for a walk. We hadn't gone far when a deer walked out in front of us on the path. I decided to turn around in case Dougal scared her. We left her in peace and I returned to the house and put Dougal in the kitchen. At this moment, something strange happened. A little voice inside me said, walk to the top of the field, and without hesitation I did. I just walked through the mist until I came to a tree. Above me, in the tree, sat the owl. She was large and beautiful, she looked at me for a bit then jumped out of the tree onto the ground in front of me. For a minute I had the incredible experience of locking eyes with a wild barn owl, before she flew silently away. I was lost in the magic of the moment, and not really listening to another little voice inside that was saying, something is wrong, this is a warning. The next day our beautiful cat Bintang disappeared. He was a long-haired beauty with the sweetest nature. This was the owl as messenger/warning animal.

As well as in real life the barn owl also came in dreams. In one very beautiful dream I found myself in a city at night, outside a pub in which I have played music many times.

I walk down an alley behind the pub, turn right and find a goddess shrine. It is open air and lit with candles and such a beautiful surprise in the city. There are chairs and people sitting around. I sit down and there is a window next to me. A white barn owl is trying to get in. I let her in and she plays with me, she is very kind. I then let her out and she sits on top of a high building looking down at me.

In another dream a woman sat with me and sang the Song of the Owl in Gaelic. The next day I did some research and found that this song actually exists. In a musical dream I learnt how to play 'owl icaros'. Icaros are the spirit songs of the Amazonian shamans. During a dream conversation with one such shaman, there was a knock at the door. I answered, to find a jaguar and a tawny owl in the doorway, they handed me a feather.

One day I turned into the lane to our house, which is about a kilometre long and to my surprise drove past a horse.

He was in good condition but had no saddle or bridle and no human with him. When I got home I told Michèle and decided to go back and check was he all right, as I was worried he might go onto the main road. When I turned around he was looking at me through the kitchen window! He then trotted through the garden into our field. I went out and the horse tentatively came to me and we gave it some carrots, apples and water. He didn't seem to be in a hurry to go anywhere, he was so beautiful to see walking in the field and I thought, *this is great, I've got a horse!* After a few hours though he began to appear restless and began to walk around the field in a certain way horses have when they are trying to get home. Eventually he walked out again through the garden and onto the path into the woods. I went after him and tried to stop him. I stood in front of him but he pushed past. I tried this a couple of times but he made it clear he had to go. I was very sad and worried as I watched him walk off into the woods but I also learnt valuable lessons about boundaries and freedom and not trying to steer the course of others on their journey home.

The horse spirit also comes to me in dreams, usually it is a black horse that bursts wildly into my consciousness, free and untameable. Once I dreamed that I made a horse amulet from copper, then I lit a fire and the horse glowed warmly in the firelight. There is so much within this simple dream. A spiritual interpretation could be that copper must be heated to make it malleable to be worked upon, just like we ourselves must surrender to the fire of spiritual purification in order to be forged into something stronger. But there is a very specific shamanic interpretation also. The horse is synonymous with the drum in shamanic tradition, it is the 'horse' we ride into the spirit worlds. In shamanic ceremony the gol, the centre, is always represented by fire. This is the way the universe via the shamanic spirits talks to the shaman, it is, in a way, a secret language of shamanism, with symbols only shamans recognise.

Of all the animal teachers that have come, perhaps the Tyrannosaurus Rex is the strangest. It is the only one that had me waking up screaming and this was because it was my shadow animal. In the first dream I found myself in a house with Michèle. The walls inside were bare brick, one of the walls was crumbling and there was a hole in the brickwork. Through this hole I could see scales and a single giant eye looking at me. I was aware of the vast weight of a dinosaur, leaning against the wall in which cracks were appearing.

In the next dream, Michèle and I were walking along a narrow path in the forest. The path was lined with T-Rex skulls, I picked one up and held it in my hands, it was gleaming white, it was beautiful to me. In another dream I'm told that there is a T-Rex skull hidden in Antarctica and that I must retrieve it. Dressed only in a t-shirt, oblivious to the cold, I go to get the skull. It is perfect, I stroke it and feel how smooth it is and have a vision of a T-Rex skull made of crystal.

The following T-Rex dreams seemed to be about it surfacing from somewhere very deep within me. I saw a cave, I saw my ancestors peaking out from inside, I was aware that from a very deep part of this cave system T-Rex was ascending. Then in another dream I saw an old wooden structure, it was part of an ancient mine. Out of the door came many of the animals that have come to me. The Tiger came out, on its back was a lion. All the animals turned to face the door, they were all scared. The Tiger and lion roared as the T-Rex emerged. That the T-Rex was about me facing the darker aspects of myself was confirmed in a very frightening dream experience.

I'm driving with Michèle in a forest. On a rise to the right in the trees I see the red kundalini serpent with the T-Rex, a stunning and scary sight. We go past and uphill. We climb through rocks and trees and come to a house. We own the house and are going to sell it. It is huge shabby and depressing. We walk through and come to a beautiful room. It is furnished Victorian style, it is a red room, the colour of the root chakra, home of kundalini. Then I leave the room and see a really long corridor with many rooms on either side, I think this may be my spine. I open a room on the right, it is small and dark I realise there is a being there, a demonic clown. It tries to kill me. It comes at me fast, I manage to catch its energy with my hands and put it out the window.

I feel in this dream the T-Rex and the cobra took me very deep inside myself to confront and purge some of my darker aspects and fears. In another dream I was in a room trying out different shamanic flutes. This somehow seemed to call the T-Rex, which manifested fully in the room with me. This was very frightening as in previous encounters I'd seen skulls, or the T-Rex from a distance, never right up next to me. It lunged at me and I dodged and ran into another room. Despite being terrified I remember observing how amazing this was, to be in a room with a real authentic ancient T-Rex. It attacked again, I dodged and the next thing, I saw it lying on the ground as if dead on the perimeter of a sacred circle. All my cats came, they were in their magical aspect, and they stood around the T-Rex. I felt sorry for the T-Rex, but I sensed it wasn't dead, the important thing was I had defeated it.

The Komodo dragon that first told me to shed my skin has also come as a dream teacher. I found myself standing next to a giant Komodo dragon. A voice said, *go and stand by the head of the dragon.* I did just this, which induced an OBE where I shapeshifted into the dragon and flew.

Mythical dragons have come too. In a beautiful early awakening dream I saw an egg of bees in the sky. Out of the bee-egg hatched a golden dragon in foetal position. It began to fall but another dragon swooped down and rescued it. I then saw the sky was full of dragons.

In another memorable dream I found myself at the top of a tall skyscraper. There were glass windows all round and I was in a room filled with hells angels, criminals and other generally unsavoury types. A dragon burst through the glass, landed in the room, sat up on its back legs and obliterated everyone with fire except me. The dragon really is a symbol of the awakened kundalini, the dormant fire serpent having grown wings and taken flight.

The feline presence has been very strong throughout this process. My own domestic cats are frequently with me in dreams and shamanic states of consciousness, I call them the ‘little bodhisattvas’. The love we have given them is always paid back ten-fold, both here and in the spirit worlds. Many cats have entered and left our lives over the years, the majority have been strays or rescue cats. I have formed such intense relationships with them and found myself nearly insane with grief when they have died or disappeared. When I first met Michèle, she had a wonderful black and white cat called Cleo. She was a real character and lived to eat. She would bite your ankles in the morning till you fed her. She would knock precious ornaments to the ground if you weren’t fast enough with the food and she could discern the sound of a tin opener a mile away. She lived to be about eighteen years old and died peacefully at home. About a year after she died she came to me in a dream. We were lying in the garden, our noses touching. She told me she loved me and I told her I loved her too. Then, a golden light surrounded us.

When we first moved to Anma, I heard a strange noise outside one morning. At first I thought it was a bird, but I went outside and to my surprise I found two cats. One was an adult black cat, the other a tiny, pure white kitten. The black cat, having brought the kitten to us, promptly disappeared, never to be seen again. I brought the kitten inside to Michèle and we were instantly in love with her, this little fluffy faerie from the woods. She was the most beautiful cat we had ever seen, we called her Akasha. She had a terrible flea infection and was very weak but we nursed her back to health and she grew into the most magnificent of cats, a long-haired beauty, she could have won any prize. Eventually though she took to spending longer and longer periods of time away from home, until one day she just didn’t come back. It seemed that she came from the forest and the forest took her back. One night soon after, I felt her lying on me, a beautiful, almost child-like female voice said, *you have been wonderful, but I have to go now*, and she was gone.

Perhaps the cat I had the deepest relationship with was Kushka, a Norwegian Forest Cat. These cats are truly very special. They are descended from semi-wild farm cats that evolved to survive in the harsh Scandinavian winters. The breed is ancient, they are known as the faerie or trollcat and in the Norse legends they pull the goddess Freya's chariot. They are quite large and have a double coat. The inner coat is woolly for insulation and the outer long and oily. Whilst the outer coat may get wet, water cannot penetrate to the inner one so the cat is really always dry. They have large hairy paws and prominent ear tufts and in fact look quite like a little lynx. These big, soft gentle cats are really great companions and Kushka was my best friend for sixteen years until he died of kidney failure. When it became clear that he was dying, I was beset with grief. Exhausted, I lay on my bed, asking the universe what would happen to him. This induced my first shamanic journey. A spiral opened in my third eye and extended into a tunnel and I went through this with my consciousness. The journey was very psychedelic with amazing colours and beautiful trees and flowers. There were messages of love written in golden light. I've no idea how long this lasted and when I came to, I was still sad, but thought, if that's where he is going, I'm happy for him. He is now a regular presence in my dreams and journeys. It is not only the cats that have passed-on, that accompany me in the spirit worlds, the ones with me today often come too, I suspect that cats naturally have a stronger connection and ability to move through the dimensions than we do, that in fact they are in a way all natural shamans. One of these in particular is Singha, a tiny Siamese stray that came to us. One day there was a knock on the door and I opened it to find my neighbour, holding a very strange looking 'Siamese' kitten. He asked was it mine and I said no, but I would gladly take it in. Singha was fat, with very short legs, a stumpy broken tail, and mad blue eyes. I thought she was magnificent! I brought her up to Michèle whom she immediately jumped on and started nuzzling. There was no fear or period of adaptation, she knew instantly that she was home, it was as if she was saying, *what took you so long to find me!* Very often I might find myself in a crazy situation in a shamanic state of consciousness, being eaten by a giant cobra or something like that. Amidst the chaos I will notice Singha is there, completely indifferent, maybe eating a mouse, just casually observing me. In fact often in my dreams of giant snakes several of my cats will be there. I'm always afraid for them, trying to get them to safety, in fear they will be eaten but the cats just don't care, they run around playing mischievously. It's quite clear that they know more than I do.

The big cats came too, lions, jaguars and lynx but one in particular made its presence felt with increasing frequency, the Tiger. It was six years however before this animal actually jumped into my third eye and began to interact with me and I understood that this was my power animal. The Tiger first showed itself in a dream that ostensibly appeared to be about a salamander.

I'm told I have to catch the salamander. I jump into a river and go deep beneath the water then come back to the surface and pull myself out, with no success in finding the salamander. Now I'm standing on the edge of a bank, it is dark and the water is now shallow. Somebody says the salamander is there but I can't see it. Eventually I put my hands blindly into the water and pull out the salamander. It is yellow with a black head, it writhes and squeals in my hands but I don't hold it tightly as I don't want to hurt it. It bites me on both hands and I can feel the poison but I don't let go. A voice tells me I must put the salamander on the right path. I think I free it in the right place, which is a straight path with paths coming off it. Then my lip swells up and is full of poison. I'm told it got in through a hole made by a tiger's claw.

Following this I had visions of tiger faces during meditation. Then I dreamed of three white tigers in a cage, I set all the tigers free. Then I saw the rubble of a collapsed house (my old life/self perhaps) and an anaconda and a white tiger moving through it together.

CHAPTER SIX

STRANGE INITIATIONS

About a year after the initial awakening, I went outside one night to admire the stars. We live high on a plateau with zero light pollution and are blessed with some magnificent night skies. I was standing in a field equidistant between two trees that grew on each side opposite each other. All the phenomena I had experienced to this point had been mostly internal and although I was ninety-nine point nine percent sure this was kundalini, there was that tiny part of me that wondered was I delusional. I asked myself, *is this REALLY kundalini?* For some reason I placed my right hand on my navel area and said out loud that classic spiritual cliché, *give me a sign.* Immediately to my left under a tree a light began to manifest about six feet in the air. It wasn't like a still point of light, it was active in constant motion and change, and it was a fiery orange in colour. It grew to the size of a metre wide sphere and then light of another quality formed around it, containing it. This light was a deep red and was completely static, no movement, it looked like a divine hand had drawn it on to this reality with a giant magic marker. Once it had grown to full size the light then moved gracefully across the field in front of me until it came to the tree on the opposite side where it curved upwards almost joyfully. It left a comet-like tail made of the 'magic marker' light behind it from its point of origin and froze like this for a few seconds, before dematerialising into thin air. Just to give you an idea of the sheer scale of this vision I went into the field the next day and measured the distance between the trees, which came to about one hundred and fifty feet. Can you picture the scene, a man standing in a starlit field between two trees, looking at a giant divine fireball with a hundred and fifty foot tail! It is truly impossible to convey the quality of the light, how absolutely not of this reality it was, how truly divine it was. It remains to this day one the most extraordinarily beautiful moments of my life and whenever life becomes difficult I remember this and KNOW, there is more and that I am loved. This event was all the more powerful as no drugs, entheogens, or altered state of consciousness were involved, non ordinary reality manifested in ordinary reality. This vision actually contained a deep message about the nature of the universe that I did not understand for years after, that the two types of light represented Shiva and Shakti. The outer static light, the great still consciousness and contained within it the active creative light of Shakti, activity contained within stillness, the enlightenment process in the human being.

Almost in a state of shock, I returned to the house and told Michèle. To her credit, after being with me for a year of kundalini awakening already, she barely batted an eyelid as high strangeness had become par for the course. It's a good test to see if someone really loves you, to relate an experience like this and it doesn't change a thing. This vision initiated a new stage of spiritual development in me. I went and sat outside on the steps and kundalini energy came on very strongly, it felt like my face was being stung by a thousand bees, a sensation that continued for a couple of days. That night in bed, kundalini moved very strongly throughout my whole body. It was very sharp and intense, incredibly pleasurable but almost to the point of pain. For a few days after I would see mini comets of silver light, about the size of tennis balls, shooting into trees.

About a year again after this, another miraculous and magical event occurred whilst I was at my mother-in-law's house in Ireland. It was the winter solstice and this normally spiritually charged day was super charged because there was also a lunar eclipse. Sometime in the early hours I awoke. I was lying on my right hand side and I could feel a presence pressing on my aura above me. I reacted as any normal person would in a room at night with something supernatural hanging over them, I said, *Oh, hello!* It seemed to be waiting for me to acknowledge it because as soon as I did, it flowed into me. This was a most strange and beautiful sensation. It flowed in through my left side, it penetrated deep into my muscles, this was actually a bit sore but in a good way. It was thick and viscous and silvery like liquid moonlight, it actually felt like the moon had melted into me. It was PURE LOVE, it is difficult to describe energy as loving but this was divine universal love beyond any human notion or expression. After a bit I sat up into a meditation position to allow the energy to flow better through me. It was kundalini but of a kind I had never experienced before, as it went up my spine it was as thick as a man's arm and my third eye bulged right out like an orange. I'm not sure how long the process took, maybe twenty minutes and when I sensed it was over I lay down again and slept. The next day I went to my sisters for Christmas dinner. It was a big family gathering and despite the fact that there was copious amounts of delicious food and good wine I ate only very lightly and abstained from alcohol, as I was aware that something very special had happened. Shortly after dinner

I began to feel ill and had to go to bed. It wasn't food poisoning as the fourteen other people there were all fine. For the next twenty-four hours I purged and purged. When not in the toilets I was lying down in great discomfort whilst this very thick kundalini moved throughout my system. I realised that this was a spiritual sickness but I did not hear about this in a shamanic context till much later. In some traditions the shaman gets ill, no medication can cure the sickness and the shaman must surrender to the process. During this time the person is spiritually modified into a person capable of being a shaman. My spiritual sickness was very short some last months, but there is no denying what it was. Spirit entered me, made me sick, purged me and altered me.

Eventually I was drawn further into the shamanic experience as life circumstances finally brought me to Peru to meet the spirit of ayahuasca, who had really been there from the beginning, as the anaconda and the jaguar.

CHAPTER SEVEN

MOTHER

I was some years into my spiritual awakening when my mother died. I would have loved to share with her my experiences, I felt she would have perhaps understood, but she was seriously ill and I didn't want to burden her. She died a long and terrible death from emphysema. She had been a life-long smoker but in all fairness she smoked the lightest of brands and didn't inhale, it seems that some people are just genetically pre-disposed to developing smoking related diseases than others. For a number of years she managed to cunningly hide her slowly worsening condition, which really came on after her retirement from being a schoolteacher. My father did hard physical work as a foreman of ground-works on the building sites, a career path followed by many Irish immigrants. This meant usually leaving the house by six in the morning, long before my mother would get up. He would bring her a cup of tea in bed then leave, not returning till the evening, usually exhausted. This gave my mother plenty of time to get her laboured breathing under control and clear her increasingly congested chest. By the time my father got home from work she had cooked dinner and had a smile on her face. He had no idea that it would have taken her most of the day to achieve this. Only when my father retired did he discover how advanced her condition was and over the space of a couple of years her condition deteriorated so much that my father became a full-time carer. Despite being in hospital occasionally with severe chest infections, she remained at home for the most part and had a team of nurses assigned to monitor her progress. My parents were of that generation where you didn't complain. Not wanting to burden my sister and I, they kept the gravity of my mother's condition hidden. We knew she was sick, just not, how sick. Towards the end of her life she was on oxygen and hunched over with severe scoliosis. Every morning she spent around three hours over a bowl trying to clear phlegm from deep in her lungs. She was sixty-nine but looked ninety-six and despite all this, she was still smoking.

Unlike some cancers, where methods of pain control are very advanced and the suffering of the patient can be reduced considerably, there was really nothing that could be done for my mother's condition. Her last months were horrific but she could always muster a smile. One morning she sat up, a surprised look came over her face and she died. I was in France and my sister called me to break the news. After the phone call I walked outside with Michèle. Standing in the field was a lone female deer; she was staring straight at us. Michèle said, *that's your mother*. A year to the day I had a dream. A deer came to me and sniffed my hand delicately, then we ran together for miles, through fields, across streams, into forests. The next day my sister called to ask how I was feeling. I had completely forgotten it was the anniversary of our mother's death. After this my mother would come to visit me more in dreams and became a sort of spirit guide to me. I first saw her in an ancient convent; she was young and beautiful and led me up spiral stairs into beautiful gardens. She had taught in convent schools and had been very happy with the nuns.

Shortly before my trip to Peru, my mother came in a very direct and powerful communication. It started as a dream where I found myself in the kitchen of a house, looking out of the window onto a large field. Two black jaguars came into the field signifying that something important was about to happen. Then my mother walked in, we hugged and went through into another larger room full of ancestors and relatives. My mother stood up and addressed us. She said - *we are a line of Indian sorcerers dedicated to fighting the evil of the Papacy*. I took this to mean the patriarchal imbalance prevalent in the world and the need to restore balance between divine male and divine female energies. After this I went up to talk to her and I became acutely aware at this point that I was talking to someone who had passed on and that this was a rare opportunity to ask some big questions. I asked her, *do we come back?* She said, *yes*. Next I asked, *will you come back?* She replied, *yes, I have things to finish.* Finally I asked, *do we have a choice?* She remained silent on this question.

CHAPTER EIGHT
AYAHUASCA

There are certain conditions that western medicine seems ill-equipped to deal with, as very often the symptoms are treated but not the cause. Within our own family we found ourselves with a life or death situation on our hands, urgent healing was needed and conventional approaches had failed miserably. One thing that comes with spiritual awakening is a desire to re-research the nature of everything you have been educated to believe, because the conditioning has been broken and the search for truth becomes paramount. This search had brought me into awareness of ayahuasca, the legendary and highly potent plant drink central to the shamanic practices of the Amazon. In recent years, ayahuasca has been shown to be particularly efficacious in curing many conditions, from diseases to addictions, that western medicine seems to be struggling with. I was convinced that our best hope lay with ayahuasca and so to this end we set off on a great healing journey to Peru. Out of respect for the privacy of other family members, I will share here only my own personal experiences during the ceremonies.

I have to say that I was very nervous about taking ayahuasca. Up to this point in my life I had never taken any mind altering substances (although they are readily available in the world of professional music), I didn't smoke cigarettes, I had never even smoked a joint, and here I was about to drink one of the most powerful hallucinogenic potions known to man!

As soon as the decision to go to Peru was made it became clear that ayahuasca knew we were coming, many signs were given and my dreams took a very shamanic twist. First a wild boar came, he was huge and terrifying but he came to me peacefully. Then I saw a pig-man facing up aggressively to a boar-man. In between these therianthropes was a green-faced shaman. I saw this as my domestic self versus my wild self, ordinary reality versus non-ordinary reality, in between these two, my shaman self. In another dream a shaman stood by my bed peering through jungle foliage with a beautiful green spider by his head.

It took a lot of research and planning to go on this ayahuasca journey but all the signs were in favour of it. I remember standing outside looking at the sky and asking, *am I doing the right thing?* The clouds formed clearly into the forms of a man and woman dancing. A couple of nights before we left for Peru I had a very shamanic dream. I saw a woodland glade; first a hare ran through it, then a deer and finally a one antlered stag. The next day my dog Dougal came into the garden with the antlers of a small deer in his mouth, I kept them, a second shamanic gift from the universe after the dragon skin. Antlers are also associated with the shedding of skin. The next morning I looked out of the bathroom window to see a stag only a few meters away in the field. I have seen deer many times, before and since, but this was the only time the stag has shown himself. The night before we were to go to the ayahuasca retreat I was sharing a hotel room with my stepson. In the early hours of the morning he woke up and said that he'd had the strangest dream. He had seen a great stag standing in a woodland glade with light shining down upon him. I knew then for sure that this was right, as I had shared nothing of my recent dreams and experiences with him.

Ayahuasca is one of the most powerful expressions of divinity on the planet and potentially one of the holiest experiences a person can have. Ayahuasca is a 'tea' (not the kind you get biscuits with!) made from the ayahuasca vine, chacruna and often a number of other plants as well, depending on the shaman's personal preference. The chacruna contains a high content of dymethletriptamime (DMT), which is the psychoactive component in the brew. It is often said that DMT is produced by the pineal gland in humans but this has not been scientifically proven yet. It has however been found in human cerebrospinal fluid and this may certainly go some way to explain why kundalini awakened people may have visionary experiences comparable to those given by ayahuasca without taking the entheogen.

Ayahuasca is an MAOI inhibiter, meaning it stops the enzyme that normally neutralises DMT in our stomachs from working. The vine itself does not contain DMT and if taken by itself does not give much of an effect but yet, it is considered the primary spiritual component of the brew. The vine itself is the medium for the spirit of ayahuasca to manifest, she is the goddess, the divine feminine expressing herself in plant spirit form and sometimes called, La Madre, The Mother. The ayahuasca vine is a wonderful example of the doctrine of signatures. She is a snake-like liana that wraps herself around a tree. This is nature expressing the kundalini around the spine and a seldom realised fact is that ayahuasca is plant kundalini, but only a kundalini awakened person familiar with the feeling of the energy and the channels it travels in the body is likely to recognise this.

Personally, I feel that the best way to enter into communion responsibly and respectfully with ayahuasca, is to undertake a dieta at the same time and adhere strictly to the restrictions imposed by the individual shaman, both before and after. There are restrictions both medical and spiritual. For us, no pharmaceutical medication, street drugs, blue cheese, alcohol, duck or pork for two weeks before. All these things can at best impede the ayahuasca from working and at worst cause an adverse reaction and kill you. The dieta involves eating lightly, very bland food with no salt or flavourings of any kind. It is essentially the original diet of the forest and enables ayahuasca to penetrate you much deeper and for much longer. In conjunction to this we also dieted trees, drinking tea made from various barks each morning. The trees are considered the biggest, most powerful spirits in the forest and they make your body an hospitable place for ayahuasca to live and also provide protection. During the dieta all sexual activity including masturbation was prohibited. We also had to avoid touching each other and mixing with the general public, as our spiritual nervous systems were wide open. After the dieta, the restrictions continued with sexual prohibition for a further month, no alcohol or drugs for a month, no pork, duck, or venison for six months. It was said that observing the restrictions allowed ayahuasca to stay with you for much longer and greatly enhanced the possibility of life changing experiences taking place. It was also a question of showing respect for the spirit of ayahuasca, breaking the dieta would at the very least stop ayahuasca from doing her work and at worst induce catastrophic life changes. It can be seen from this that entering into communion with ayahuasca is no small commitment and not one to be taken lightly. Dieta is how Amazonian shamans become shamans. I use the word shaman here only for convenience, it is not used in Peru where words like curandero, ayahuascero or vegetalista describe these traditional healers. Repeated dietas with different plants, in total seclusion, for extended periods of time are undertaken. Each plant may lead the shaman to another and on and on. The more dieta a shaman does the more power they have. It is said that ayahuasca taken just once in combination with dieta is one hundred times more powerful than taking ayahuasca a hundred times without.

For our first ayahuasca ceremonies we travelled to a retreat centre called The Way Inn. This is a mountain lodge situated in the Andes at very high altitude. The setting is spectacularly beautiful and the presence of the great mountain spirits, the Apus, is palpable. Ayahuasca is taken at night in the dark and we all gathered in the ceremony room around six pm. We each had a mattress to lie on, a plastic bowl to throw up in, a bottle of water to rinse our mouths (you can't swallow water, it's just to get rid of the taste which is absolutely foul) and a blanket, because at times ayahuasca can make you very cold indeed. The mattresses were arranged in a circle with the shaman and the mesa at the top. The mesa (table) is a collection of objects; stones, crystals, skulls, feathers, statues, all sorts of things of spiritual significance both traditionally and to the shaman personally. It is the centre of power and protection in the ceremony.

Our shaman was Maestro Gumercindo or Gumé for short. By candlelight he poured ayahuasca into a small cup and sang or whistled an icaro into the cup with special intention placed on the person to drink. The icaros are magical healing songs, either passed from shaman to shaman or learned directly from plant spirits. Gumé's icaros are incredibly beautiful and remain with me still. Once Gumé had finished singing, the person would come forward to take the cup. Before drinking you must put your intention into the cup, what you hope to get from the journey. Once done, you say *Salud!* and drink. Everyone answers back *Salud!* Everyone drinks from the same cup. I was about halfway through the circle, and I watched with increasing nervousness as my turn approached. When my turn came I took the cup and simply said, *teach me what I need to know.* The foul taste of ayahuasca is almost as legendary as its effects but to my surprise it actually tasted quite pleasant, I felt no need to wash out my mouth and I wondered why so many complained about the taste. This was the only time ayahuasca was to taste pleasant. The taste got increasingly worse with each ceremony, so much so that by the end of the retreat I was actually almost vomiting before I took it!

The ayahuasca experience is different for everyone. One of her aspects is that she is a spiritual cleaner; she goes through all the chakras and nadis cleaning them out. This is exactly what kundalini does, in fact it has been suggested that one cup of ayahuasca is the equivalent of ten years meditation.

Before ayahuasca can bring the visionary aspect to a person she must do this cleaning but some people need so much cleaning that they need to take ayahuasca many times before having visuals.

About fifteen minutes after drinking I began to feel what they call ‘mareado’. Your body feels drunk but your mind is crystal clear. We had been told to sit up for as long as possible but I just had to lie down. Soon the shaman began singing and shaking his leaf rattle and I began to hear the strange buzzing machine like noises that sometimes precede the onset of visions. Then I felt the ayahuasca travel up my spine just like kundalini. I knew she was heading for my pineal gland. As she got closer I saw a beautiful magical being shoot a ray of pure white light into my third eye. My third eye unfolded like a blue flower and then I was inside my pineal gland. It was like being inside a giant blue pinecone shaped cathedral and then I went out through the top. I was shown a tube or tunnel made of circles of golden light, I could see the blue human soul ascending through this.

At some point I began to feel a stirring deep within me and realised this was the onset of the purgation for which ayahuasca is so famous. I could see a python patterned with bile green and yellow, very bright, luminous, forming in my intestines, it then began to rise. As its head approached my trachea I knew I had to get to my bucket and I turned on my belly and reached for it. In normal consciousness the bucket was about one foot away from me but in ayahuasca consciousness it was about ten feet away. I crawled what seemed to be an impossibly long distance and finally managed to grasp my bowl, the problem now was it had grown so big that I could barely get my arms around it. Finally, just in time I got positioned over my bowl for the big event. At this point I noticed that there was a tunnel in my bowl going down to eternity and there was a face in this tunnel and that face was mine. You can't deny the universe has a sense of humour when a spiritual purge involves vomiting on your own face! The purging was truly wondrous, I didn't bring up much food because of dieta but I could feel things coming up from very deep inside me, poisonous things, dark things, fears, negative thoughts and emotions, I wondered how such evil could ever have lived inside me. I lay down again and the visions returned. I was shown ancient temples, Mayan, Incan, and Toltec. I was shown the intricate carvings on the walls and I sensed I was being shown something important to do with our origins. At one point I went to the toilet, the light was on and I could see spirit anacondas flying all around me.

The next day I was very happy to have survived ayahuasca and was looking forward to the next ceremony. One of the organisers told me that ayahuasca is often wonderful the first time, it's kind of a nice hello, but after that she gets down to some serious work with you, and this indeed proved to be the case.

The next night after drinking I went very quickly into an incredibly disturbing state of consciousness. It was blue and vast and intelligent beyond human comprehension. Somehow I knew this state was Shiva. There were no actual visions with my eyes closed, just this alien state of mind. It was so scary I thought I was either going to die or go insane or both. I didn't think I could come back from this without a shattered mind. I found myself gripping the mattress as this was the only evidence I had that I wasn't dead and still in this world. Sometimes in an attempt to verify I wasn't dead I would open my eyes but immediately visions would form in the room, which I sensed would be terrifying. I did not keep my eyes open long enough to see what they were as I felt that at some level I could accept this state of consciousness in my head but I could not accept it outside my head as well without cracking up, so I chose to believe that outside was still normal, a bit. After several hours in this state the ayahuasca began to wear off and I fell into the deepest of sleeps. The next morning I felt I could not drink ayahuasca again, I really felt that I could not endure another experience like this and survive. However, it is said that the time that you really don't want to go into ceremony again is the time you really should. It's only the ego saying no because it doesn't like what's being done to it. In retrospect I feel that during that ceremony I was being offered ego death but I wasn't ready to accept it. By mid afternoon, I was feeling better and to my surprise felt ready to enter ceremony again. The next ceremony was rather unorthodox as instead of traditional icaros we used mantra instead. The holiness of mantra becomes fully apparent under ayahuasca and the ceremony was beautiful as mantra after mantra moved through me. In my first journey I found myself in the centre of the hollow earth, I could see the continents on the outside of the globe. Then a portal opened into to space and millions of stars rushed towards me or I rushed towards them, I'm not sure. I found myself in space and all the stars were pouring into my crown chakra. Then I saw Shiva. He was a most beautiful luminous blue; he rested his great head on a mountain range, behind him a deep black night sky. Huge shooting stars were pouring into his head, then into me and I merged with Shiva. My next ceremony was very important in my shamanic path as I feel that it was then that aspects of my shamanic self were awoken. First I saw an Angel, in the form of a column of light, angelic wings stretched out from either side of it. Then I was shown the Holy Grail. It rested on a carved white stone pedestal, again, angel wings spread out from either side. Then I found myself standing in a great canyon. I saw a bird with a carved wooden totem pole head above me, and then eagles and condors flew around me. I saw a great stag and fell asleep in the arms of a bear.

After these first ceremonies in the Andes, we then journeyed to visit ayahuasca in her true home, the Amazon rainforest. To this end, we headed to the city of Iquitos. Iquitos is the only city in the world located inside a rainforest. There are no roads in; it is accessible only by plane or through an arduous boat journey. To get there we were to fly first to Lima then get a connecting flight. However, a passenger fell ill on the first flight resulting in the plane being diverted to Iquitos for an emergency stop. It was great testament to the skill of the pilot that he landed this huge aircraft in this absolutely tiny third world airport equipped only for much smaller planes. It was six thirty in the morning but frustratingly we were not allowed to disembark but had to carry on to Lima. In Lima we actually nearly missed our flight to get back to the airport where we had been sitting that morning!

Iquitos is a small city, quite run down but with hints of past colonial glory. Most of the ayahuasca centres are in close proximity and as such it is really a kind of 'Ayahuasca Central'. It is also the strangest place on Earth. The spiritual energy is palpable in Iquitos, a raw magic emanating from the heart of the rainforest where plant spirit shamanism has been practised in unbroken tradition for thousands of years. The first night in the hotel Michèle had a huge dream re-living the death of her mother. I dreamed I was escorting entities out of the room. Just a short walk from our hotel was a cafe where all the westerners would hang out and talk about ayahuasca, retreat centres and each other. We quickly realised that this was a place where everyone knew everything about everyone else. Yet it was also very seductive, the type of place that might take hold of you, that you might never leave. We got talking to an American man who ran an ayahuasca and huachuma retreat. He was a great raconteur and regaled us with some wild tales of doing ceremonies up in the ancient temple complex of Chavin de Huantar. We remarked upon the energy of Iquitos and he laughed saying sometimes he felt like it was a kind of purgatory, that everyone in Iquitos was actually dead and that you came here before being shipped off to your respective Heaven or Hell. I began to feel as if I was in a Stephen King novel, that in fact our plane had crashed in Iquitos and the sick woman that was taken off was actually the only survivor and the rest of us were dead! A beggar walked past and our friend gave some money. He turned to us and said, *always best to be on the safe side, you never know who might be an angel in disguise in Iquitos.*

Our next retreat centre was Dreamglade, about a two-hour drive outside the city. It was very beautiful, no electricity, simple traditional tambos and a large central maloka for ceremonies. All this built around a large lake, inside thirty-five acres of rainforest. The feeling of being in the rainforest was exquisite, I felt like I was at the centre of the world, that I was part of the forest and the forest part of me, that there were spirits everywhere.

Our 'shaman' was a Shipibo woman called Estella. She had had her first visionary experiences aged five and could tell not only when people were pregnant before they knew it themselves, but also the sex of the child they were going to have. She trained with her grandmother for twelve years, dieting countless plants and considered herself to be a 'vegetalista'. I asked her could she see our energy fields at all times or just when she had taken ayahuasca. She said she could see everything at all times because she had dieted Toé. Toé is one of the BIG plants in the Amazonian tradition and Estella had dieted it for a year. In ceremony, she had no mesa or leaf rattle. She had some bags of various medicinal plants and some agua florida beside her, but that was it. She also rarely moved from her place in ceremony unless someone was really suffering. She remained where she was and the healing power emanated out into the ceremony from her. Her icaros were powerful and relentless; it felt as if no sickness or negativity could resist them. Sometimes it felt as if she was leaning right over me singing in my ear, but she never moved from her place. She said that when she had ayahuasca inside her, she had the cure to all the diseases in the world.

In our previous ceremonies we had drunk cielo ayahuasca mixed with chacruna, sanango and mapacho. This ayahuasca was quite different. This was black ayahuasca. It was mixed with chacruna and another plant, chaliponga, which contains fifteen percent more DMT than chacruna, so it was a very potent brew. Estella said that the balance between leaf and vine was excellent and that it was very good medicine.

It was late and we were very tired upon getting to the retreat and we just had time to change before going straight into ceremony. I wasn't ready for a big ayahuasca experience that night so I drank just a quarter of a cup. I'm very sensitive to ayahuasca and wanted to just dip my toe in the water so to speak, to test the strength of the medicine. The ayahuasca was very thick, I got a slight honey taste from it. In fact, to me it almost tasted nice which is very unusual for ayahuasca. The effects came on quite fast, I saw Shipibo patterns, snakes and pure white light. It was a very relaxing, peaceful ceremony with no purging and just what I needed. The next day I had a vision of a huge anaconda swimming in the lake and two bluebirds flying around it.

The following day was to bring with it some of the most profound spiritual experiences of my life. First we began our dieta. This time we were dieting ajos sacha. Its name means false garlic and it does have a very strong garlic smell. It has many healing properties and also contributes to clarity of mind and focus. Everyday we would drink a glass of it. We would also receive it as a plant bath; water with the leaves macerating in it would be poured over our heads and bodies whilst prayers were said. This also acted as protection in the ayahuasca ceremonies.

That afternoon there was the opportunity to do a tobacco purge. I was initially quite reluctant, as I had seen a person get very ill because they had failed to purge all the tobacco from their system. Also, the abuse of tobacco within my family had created an emotional barrier, even though I knew that in the Amazon it was a very important sacred plant medicine. It is said that ayahuasca loves tobacco. I initially said no but my intuition was strongly pushing me towards doing the purge so in the end I went with my heart instead of my head and I'm so glad I did. The purge itself involves drinking a large glass of concentrated tobacco juice. You let this rest in your stomach for a few minutes then you start drinking warm water, A LOT of water. We were each given a large basin full. The type of basin you use for doing the washing up, it's like drinking a sink full of water very fast. You keep drinking until the vomiting begins and the tobacco mixed with water shoots out of your mouth in great streams. At one point I was in difficulty but the shaman came along and rubbed my stomach and I was off again. You keep drinking until all the tobacco is out and you can drink without vomiting. By the time I'd finished I was completely drenched, I'd sweated right through my shirt but I felt amazing, I mean really amazing, superhuman. I was advised to have a swim followed by some rest before ceremony. The medicine had penetrated me deeply and lying in my tambo I was filled with blissful sensations, particularly in my legs and the spirit of tobacco rocked me gently. Also some curious processes were initiating in my stomach, it felt like a giant spoon was gently stirring my insides round and round. It was all so beautiful I was laughing out loud and tearful at the same time. Recently there were sensationalist headlines in the papers concerning the tragic death of a young woman at an ayahuasca retreat in Peru. Although all the facts were far from clear, a tobacco purge was given as the likely cause of death and the usual fear mongering ensued, this time centering around tobacco instead of ayahuasca, as is usually the case. I found it ironic and absolutely typical of western media that although we have been killing ourselves for years, by the millions, through tobacco abuse, one death, in a country that's been using it for millennia as a healing medicine gets a headline.

Between being on dieta and having done the tobacco purge I felt wonderfully clean and empty going into ceremony that night. I felt confident and ready to take whatever ayahuasca wanted to throw at me and I drank a half-cup, which is a big dose for me. I then settled down on my mattress to await what the ceremony would bring. Initially though, it seemed to take a long time for the ayahuasca to take effect, which seemed strange because the night before I had taken less ayahuasca but felt the effects very quickly. Then again sometimes you think you are not mareado when you actually are. I saw very clearly the face of a blue deity, but after this nothing. In fact I felt so un-mareado that I decided to sit up with a straight spine in meditation position. I immediately then felt the ayahuasca coming on very fast and strong and had to lie down straight away. Vast snake-like coils began to engulf the room all around me. Sometimes with ayahuasca the visionary aspect can be like watching a film in your third eye. With the stronger experience you are inside the vision and the 'real' world is subsumed, this was one such occasion. The vast coils began to morph into different shapes, textures and colours and I was aware of being inside the creative power of the universe, that place of infinite manifestation and possibility, the place from which all form pours forth and solidifies into the material world. This was the veiling, concealing power of Shakti, from this state the illusion of separation, the matrix is created. For a time I went very deep into this state, which I can't deny was a little scary. Following this however I found myself surrounded by hundreds of green snakes, which flowed all around me, making me feel very blissful.

During the ceremonies, at some point, each person would be taken up to sit in front of Estella for a limpieza. This is a personal healing, where she works on cleaning your energy and inducing any disease to purge. It is a very powerful experience having the icaro sung right into you. Some people just vomit instantly; it can be very difficult to even sit up. When it came to Michèle's turn to go up, I was really concentrating on sending her loads of love and hoping she was having a good ceremony with the healing she needed. As I was doing this I felt myself going very deep again and I became aware of something vast forming in the air to my left hand side. I realised that what I was looking at was actually my own spine. Little, different coloured lights began to come on from the bottom to the top; it looked a bit like a runway. As the lights were coming on in my spine I felt kundalini entering at the sacrum, a delicious heat moved up my body, my hands and fingers stretched out and my head began to shake as powerful energy came into my pineal gland. My left nostril then became incredibly clear and I began to take true yogic breaths, I could feel the breath coming from deep down travelling all the way up through the nadi. At this point I realised I was being given the great gift of a second kundalini awakening.

My tongue now began to take on a life of its own and enter into spontaneous kechari mudra. Kechari mudra is a very advanced yoga technique, which perhaps only a handful of people in the world have ever entered into. The Yoga Kundalini Upanishad states that,

> *'The knowledge of Khechari is rare and also rare is its practice.' 13*

and that, Kechari means *'to fly through inner space'*. There is a chakra on the tip of the tongue and in advanced stages of kundalini awakening the tongue begins to curl back in the mouth. It is seeking the area behind the soft palate at the nasal pharynx. This highly sensitive area is the casing of the pineal gland. When the chakra on the tip of the tongue touches this point a state of full body energetic union occurs.

> *'The mind moves in space; the tongue enters space. Therefore the name kechari was chosen by the masters for this mudra.'14*

It is in this space that the confluence of ida, pingala and sushumna occurs. It is difficult to convey just how 'big', how important kechari mudra is. Both the Yoga Kundalini Upanishad and the Hatha Yoga Pradipika talk about it in exalted language.

'There is only one seed, pervading creation; one mudra, Khechari; one God, independent;one state, manonmani.' 15

My tongue had been going back to the soft palate in meditation for quite sometime although I had not yet reached full kechari, as my tongue isn't long enough. There are various tongue lengthening measures that can be employed but aside from this the kechari process may take years, as a very purified spiritual nervous system is needed to be able to cope with it. In this instance however ayahuasca took over the show and she was in full Vedic/yogic mode. She pulled my tongue back to the soft palate, then I felt and could see kundalini energy streaming out of the tip of my tongue, curling up behind the nasal pharynx and shoot straight into my pineal gland. Then my tongue seemed to disappear, a crystal of violet light appeared in the centre of my head, waves of pure consciousness swept over me, into me, and I entered into 'yoga', into union. There are really no words to describe the beauty of this samadhi state. Time ceased to exist so I have no idea how long it lasted. Eventually I found myself within the coils of a vast anaconda. Her patterns were lit up with many beautiful tiny lights and through the centre of her coils was the white light of pure consciousness. I knew I was being shown the true nature of the universe. The anaconda as Shakti, enfolding us in the coils of the matrix illusion of unlimited manifestation and possibility. The white light the eternal unchanging consciousness, Shiva, who enters into the illusion of separation to 'play' in the coils of Maya. I knew that when we are tired of 'playing' we go through into that white light.

When it came to my turn to sit in front of Estella I was in a very high vibrational state and my body began to move in rhythm with her icaro. My tongue was continuing to go up in kechari and then something miraculous happened, I tasted a thick, sticky sweet substance on the tip of my tongue. I brought it down into my mouth, tasted some more, swallowed and was immediately filled with bliss. To my sheer amazement I realised, I was tasting amrita, the legendary nectar of the gods. The production of amrita occurs as part of the nectar cycle in the kundalini awakened person's body. Certain mysterious processes go on in the stomach, as digestion plays a very important role in the process. The oldest of the Vedas, the Rig Veda, talks about churning the vats of soma and drinking the soma. This has led to speculation that soma was some kind of entheogen. In my opinion this is not the case and that 'churning the vats of Soma' refers to this very process, when I felt that 'giant spoon' turning in my stomach this was what I was feeling, the soma in pre-amrita stage. This process then combines with the cerebrospinal fluid and is transformed in the brain into amrita, which drips down the back of the throat. This is partly why the tongue goes back in kechari, because it wants to taste the amrita. Via the tongue the amrita is distributed through the body in a different way than through just swallowing. I would taste the amrita then swallow and every time I did I was filled with joy and bliss, I felt it all through my body. The Upanishads attribute miraculous qualities to this soma.

> *'The knower of Yoga-tongue above, steady drinking soma-undoubtedly conquers death...' 16*

'As the fire, the fuel, and the flame, the oily wick, so the soul does not abandon a body filled with drops of soma.' 17

When I returned to my place I sat up in meditation position and a whole set of kriyas ensued. In particular my sacrum would shake very rapidly and my head would roll grinding my neck bones. This seemed to go on for some time until all the vertebrae in my spine cracked from bottom to top and my spine was completely re-aligned. The amrita continued to flow for several hours, filling me with such bliss I was grinning like a Cheshire cat! I can only describe the sense of this whole experience as 'Vedic' and it further confirmed for me the truth to be found in the ancient Sanskrit texts and the yogic/tantric systems of spiritual practice.

The next day, despite still feeling very blissful I had a slight ache in my stomach. I was virtually empty of food at this stage and I suspected that there was still something in me to purge, despite the fact that the shaman had told me I was the 'cleanest' person in the group. Also, there was something very strange, I felt like I had sand in my mouth. It was grinding between my teeth and no matter how much I cleaned them it still kept coming back and no one could give me an explanation for this. Everything would become clear to me in the next ceremony, which proved to be one of my most rewarding but also most difficult.

In this ceremony, after drinking the ayahuasca, I lay down and got comfortable on my mattress. I had just achieved a level of perfect comfort (which is a big thing for me as I'm a great fidgeter), when I heard something jump off the wall of the maloka and got quite a fright when it landed on my head! It was pitch black so I couldn't see what it was but I was convinced it was a tarantula and I sat up brushing my hair frantically. During the rest of the ceremony this mysterious beastie continued to make its presence felt and I began to think it must be there for a reason.

I lay down again and let the ayahuasca come, I became aware of the roots of a vast brown plant surrounding me and permeating me. This part of the ceremony was very joyful. I lay on my back and my hands began to flap up and down on the mattress. I began to laugh and felt my hands becoming infused with spiritual energy, something I would need later on in the ceremony.

Soon, the ache in my stomach became more noticeable and I sensed something coming to the surface. As the shaman began to sing I began to cough and spit. It was a dry cough with very little physical substance coming out. The coughing and spitting increased and the mareado state became very strong. My nose then also began to purge and I was aware of something very deep emerging. I began to realise that I was beginning to purge two diseases that have afflicted me since childhood, an asthmatic condition and chronic rhinitis. For me, the ayahuasca purge is always a very multi-dimensional experience. Whatever I am purging begins to manifest around me. I see zigzag patterns, lurid colours, jarring energy; I can see and feel what is in me being pulled out by ayahuasca. I began to purge from deep down in my intestines, I could feel something wriggling inside me. With a great effort I brought it up and a snake slithered out of my mouth into my bowl and disappeared, but there was much more to come. As the purge progressed I began to sense that it was connected to tobacco, the tobacco purge I had done earlier had initiated contact with this great plant teacher. The purge continued to deepen and I realised that not only was I healing myself but my mother also, it felt as if I was actually taking her sickness and getting rid of it. The purge and state of mareado became so intense that Estella left her place and sat with me, soothing me with flower water and energetically cleansing me. I told the diseases I loved them and thanked them for their lessons and asked them to go into the light. Deep in mareado, my left hand would repeatedly come to my forehead and make a cross sign, it almost felt as if I was anointing my pineal gland. Lying on my front over my bowl, ayahuasca would rock my hips and stomach, churning and churning up the disease. This went on for a couple of hours until I felt I might also need to go to the toilet. Sitting on the toilet holding my bowl in my hands the mareado state got even stronger and I was getting weaker. I wasn't sure I could take much more and called for Estella to see if she could help but she said I had to go through it alone. Normally with ayahuasca you don't drink water but now I knew that I had to drink and that in fact I was doing another tobacco purge, that the healing spirit of tobacco was healing me of tobacco abuse. I drank pints and pints of water. Throughout all this Estella's assistant, a young American man named Drew, took great care of me. I went very deep with the disease, I could see it within me, at one point I was so deep I stopped breathing. I heard Drew say, *don't forget to breath buddy!* I actually felt oneness with the sickness, I understood it wasn't bad, it just was what it was. Hard as the process was, I found myself laughing during much of it and giving thanks that the disease was leaving me. My nose was also purging throughout this, I would blow, flush the tissue away and say, *go away and come back as something nice*. Sometimes the disease would come into my hands. I was able to hold them over the bowl and 'brush' it off. My hands would continue this brushing action until they were energetically clean, at this point they would come together in prayer position. What was coming out was so toxic that if I accidently touched the contents of the bowl it felt almost radioactive. Drew was brilliant throughout this process, giving me cleansing agua florida of tobacco and blowing cooling tobacco smoke over me. Finally I felt stillness, I again sensed a Vedic presence, I was filled with violet light in geometric patterns, and just like that, the disease was gone and I was back! I later discovered that Drew had helped me by taking a small part of my sickness into himself which was such a truly selfless act. The next day he too had sand in his mouth.

Just as upon arriving in Iquitos, I had had strange dreams, the same happened upon leaving. First I had a vision of the jungle in which appeared the face of a native woman with beautiful eyes, La Madre I think. On my last night in Iquitos I dreamed of an ancient mound in the jungle. It was used for ceremonies and it was my job to make sure it was clear and safe from giant sloths. I realised this was a memory of a past life many millennia ago when humans and *megatherium* existed together. As I watched, giant sloths moved slowly away from the mound. Just before the winter solstice the giant sloth came back. In this dream I walked into a museum, the concrete floor cracked open and a giant sloth emerged. It nuzzled and cuddled me. Curious as to the possible message of this huge, extinct power animal I did some research and all I could find about the spiritual meaning of the giant sloth was in, 'Mysteries of the Jaguar Shamans of the North-West Amazon', by Robin M. Wright. In western Amazonia, despite being extinct (probably) for thousands of years, the giant sloth is an avatar for the creation god Kuwai. Like Kuwai, the sloth is capable of living in several worlds at different moments of the seasonal cycle. Its actions of ascending and descending trees recalls perfectly the actions of the spirit of initiation, Kuwai. The giant sloth, megatherium was actually a ground dwelling animal but its great size allowed it to reach to the highest branches, in this sense it links the elements of earth and air. It walked with its great claws facing inwards, not outwardly aggressive yet showing immense power.

After Iquitos we travelled on to Cusco for a time before going home. In Cusco there was the opportunity to do one more ayahuasca ceremony. I was slightly reluctant as I didn't feel comfortable with the shaman. I even received a warning dream confirming this but at the end the Jaguar came and I was filled with a feeling of joy. My intuition told me to go ahead with the ceremony but with open eyes. That night there was only my stepdaughter and myself in the ceremony. We drank black ayahuasca mixed with chacruna, it was very nice tasting and proved to be excellent, unlike the shaman who confirmed my earlier suspicions. Quite early on in the ceremony after half-heartedly singing a couple of icaros he fell asleep and started snoring loudly. I found this quite funny but my stepdaughter got quite cross and despite being mareado got up and made enough noise to wake him up. He woke with a start and frantically began whistling an icaro, wondering if he had been caught. Later I could here him rummaging through a bag pulling things out. One moment he was banging a drum, the next playing a jaw harp. By the time he got to the glockenspiel I was convinced he was trying to mess with my mind. It was hilarious, I half expected him to pull out a set of bagpipes. Fortunately, for most of the night we were left alone with the ayahuasca. This was actually quite strange as we were used to being in ceremonies where icaro were sung almost constantly and it was very different being in a deep visionary state but without the icaros to guide us, only silence. This ceremony seemed very long, I didn't purge but the ayahuasca was quite relentless and waves and waves of visions came to me for many hours. We both experienced a black energy, it was blacker than the darkness of the maloka. It didn't however seem negative, but all the same I didn't allow it full manifestation or interaction with me and 'blew' it away. The visions felt far more traditionally shamanic than Vedic this time. First I saw beautiful snakes and then the tunnel opened up before me and the Jaguar came. I knew it would, as I had dreamed about it the night before. After this I saw my consciousness again change into a crystalline structure as it had also in one of the jungle ceremonies. More snakes came and I reached out and pulled a huge black one towards me, I felt its coils envelope me, then move through me. I saw trees with mystical designs painted on them. The most wonderful moment was seeing the Tiger with absolute clarity; it appeared so clearly, such a beautiful face, eyes full of love and compassion. I knew that this Tiger loved me and I felt the same. At one point I felt a sort of jolt at the back of my head just below my crown chakra and found myself looking at a full moon in my third eye. I understood that something important had happened, that I was now in awareness of the bindu chakra and that it was open. The bindu chakra is considered the point of emanation and retraction of consciousness; those that have 'pierced' the bindu have reached the highest state of awareness. It is said to resemble a round box. With its lid slightly ajar, light emanates from it, creating a crescent moon lying on its back. When fully opened it is perceived as a full moon. The bindu can be felt at the back of the head below the crown, the point where Hare Krishnas have their ponytail. Awareness of it has been permanent since this ceremony. The bindu chakra is associated with the production of soma/amrita, which is expressly connected to the moon in the Hatha Yoga Pradapika.

> *'Divine liquor is the essence that flows from the moon.' 18*
> *'It is truly Shiva's beloved. Cover the unequalled, divine sushumna at the back opening where the stream flows from the moon.' 19*
> *'Salutations to you, Sushumna, kundalini, nectar born of the moon, manomani, great power in the form of consciousness.' 20*

The next morning something quite magical happened and I suspect this was the whole reason for our being there. It was about six in the morning and we sat outside the maloka talking. We were high above Cusco and all was quiet, no traffic noise, just us. My stepdaughter was starting to relate to me the story of how a hummingbird had flown right up to her the day before. She had barely said the word 'hummingbird' when a large bird came down fast from high in the sky, flew in between us and fluttered all over her face. It then shot off into some nearby trees. She had received a direct blessing from Spirit.

CHAPTER NINE

FIRST DRUM

'...the shaman drum comes to us by the destiny of the spirits...' Sarangerel

Upon returning to Europe I adhered strictly to the post dieta restrictions and ayahuasca continued to do her work, bringing me slowly towards a more shamanic state of being and I began to have dreams of drums and drumming. I felt no real connection with shamanic drumming knew nothing about it and didn't really search for any deep meanings in these dreams. Repeatedly I would dream of being in drum circles, sometimes with people from the retreat. Eventually I was given a dream that I couldn't ignore. In the dream I found myself outside a shamanic drum shop. There were dozens of beautiful drums in the windows. I went inside and found that there was a woman giving a class on shamanic drumming. I sat down next to her and told her all about myself. She said, *we will have to find you a teacher.*

She called a tall man over to us. He was wearing an animal mask made of light. It was incredibly beautiful as the light was in constant movement and changing through all the colours of the spectrum. After this all I could hear through the night was drumming.

The next day I took the hint and resolved to get a drum. I soon realised that the best approach by far was to make my own, as personal involvement would make for a much deeper spirit connection. I obtained a beautiful red deer stag hide; it was a by-product from an organic deer farm where the animals are well treated. Stag felt perfect as I had dreamed of the one horned stag, seen the stag in the field and Dougal had brought me antlers. For the hoop I chose Oak; in this way, although the drum was to be in the lacing style found often in North America and also Siberia it would be firmly rooted in the European forest. I made the drum in a ceremony, which was a very rewarding experience. The hoop was the bone/skeleton of the stag and onto this was painted red ochre for the blood. Then, the hide of course is the skin and when you have put this on, you have effectively recreated the animal in a symbolic manner. I did this, and then spent time meditating, connecting with and sending love to the stag and the oak. That night I dreamed I was in a train. Two children wearing animal masks made of light danced in front of me in my carriage; I took this to be approval from the spirits. A year or so later I helped Michèle make her own drum. This one was slightly smaller than mine made from fallow deer skin with beautiful markings and a hornbeam hoop, a tree associated with witches. Nature gave approval, as seven red kites flew above us. When we'd finished we went back into the kitchen and a praying mantis dropped from the ceiling onto Michèle's head, further signalling the presence and approval of the spirits.

CHAPTER TEN

TRAIL OF SPIRIT

During my first ayahuasca retreat I made everyone laugh when I came out of mareado and declared, *I have awoken with strange devotion to Shiva!* I didn't understand why ayahuasca was repeatedly taking me to Shiva, as I had no real affinity with, or knowledge of this deity. Now I see more clearly. Shiva wears an animal skin, he dances, he has a drum, he has an entheogen in his hair, he is a super-shaman!

In Buryat shamanic tradition the principle spirit of the shaman is called the udha. The udha bonds with the shaman and is responsible for the acquisition of power animals and the initial calling of the shaman. Within Buryat cosmology, there is the World River, in which all times and consciousnesses merge. A tributary of this river is the sunsii mur, the 'trail of spirit', which is the collective memory of all the shamans, the udha has ever bonded with and will bond with in the future. I had been feeling some confusion as shaman spirits were coming to me from various different cultures, none of which were my own. Sarangerel explained however, that the udha can actually seem like a collection of spirits, even though in reality it is only one. This made perfect sense to me and explained the many different shamans I was encountering. I am however not Mongolian and don't feel comfortable with the word udha, I just think of it as my personal shamanic spirit, in many guises.

One of the first shamans to come to me was an elephant. I saw him in the garden of my old house in Ireland. He sat down in front of me, he wore a covering of leaves all over his body, I just 'knew' he was a shaman. In another dream I stood next to an African shaman. He handed me an egg, it was vibrating with possibility. This period concluded with a terrifying initiation. A giant African shaman came, my head barely reached his waist, he was solid as stone, immovable. He showed me a row of skulls with rotting flesh and hair hanging from them. He held my head in a vice like grip, I fought but it was futile, I was powerless in his grip. He forced me to eat blood, bone, hair and flesh from these skulls.

Later, my dreams took a turn towards Native -American spirituality and medicine men began to come. In one dream I was sitting by the banks of a river playing my pipes. A medicine man came and sat by me and said he wanted to play music with me but first I had to go with him. He then took me to a special place and said, *from here you can access all the directions*. This was a direct shamanic teaching concerning the four directions, the point from which they can all be accessed being the gol, the centre, which is within you, wherever you are. Another time a medicine woman came and gave me a mushroom to chew and within the dream I began to hallucinate. Then a medicine man came and took my hands. He placed his fingers and thumbs on pressure points and sang me a beautiful healing song. I woke up full of joy.

One dream felt like it was almost a review of my spiritual progress. One minute I was walking along with a medicine man and rolling my drum along in front of me. Then I found myself in a circular room. I decided to get up and pull the curtains but when I got to the wall I realised that I was actually inside my drum. I turned to find that the medicine man and an old female Siberian shaman were sitting on the floor. The woman was in trance. I sat down with them and we talked. I can't remember much, only that the medicine man said, *we can come back here again if we need to.*

In a very beautiful dream I saw a door in a rock with the head of a medicine man carved above it. I went through it into a cave, with my drum. In the darkness a Native-American healing song came from inside my drum vibrating through me in the cave. I walked outside again and many crows flew by, someone said it was a great blessing. I realised that I was on a reservation, I heard beautiful music, everyone was singing in praise of creation.

Finally, shamans from the far north, from Siberia and from the Sami began to make their presence felt. They guided me in the making of two more drums, which I talk about in detail later on. They told me, *you are here to make drums, not the kind that make noise, but those that take you to the centre of the universe.* In other words, drums that can take you to the gol, the true source of all shamanic power. Sometimes, at the start of a shamanic journey, a shaman will hold a drum in front of me. With a magical gesture from his hand a spiral tunnel will open in the face of the drum, and I go through.

Eliade observed that in many cases the spirits would make modifications to the shaman by placing objects such as crystals inside them. At this stage this began happening to me and many times spirit shamans would throw or pour things into me.

I see a shaman with a drum and hear it sounding like a heartbeat. I go down a tunnel and meet with a huge snake. A being of light comes, it is floating, holding a sphere of light in its hands like a planet, it places the sphere in my heart.

I find myself on the couch with an anaconda nuzzling me. I am given ayahuasca and we go to a dark ascent. I go up steep stairs, it's very hard to move my legs. Fractal patterns appear. When I reach the top a spirit is there. He draws a circle of light on my forehead with his finger and opens my third eye. I then come fully conscious. He holds up a tiny circular object between thumb and forefinger. It's like a pearl; he throws it into my third eye.

It is normal sometimes to have doubts about our spiritual process and experience; to ask ourselves is it important, how does it impact the world in a positive way. My sense of impotence in the face of the corruption of our governments, of the horrors inflicted on the environment and the appalling way we treat our fellow Earthlings was addressed in the following dream by a shaman child.

I find myself in a house with a child with feathers in his hair, a child shaman. We go upstairs to a room full of world leaders, Michèle Obama is head of the table, and George Bush is slumped drunk, asleep in a corner. The agenda is to kill all the wolves. I'm angry and stand up, I try to appeal to Michèle Obama but she can't hear me. There is a creepy old woman behind her sucking her finger and this gives her complete control of Michèle, I understand her to represent the dark spiritual presence controlling many of those in power.

All the time the shaman child, invisible to all but me, just keeps dancing sunwise around the table, as if to say 'don't worry, all you can do is keep on doing the shaman dance'.

The deep ecologist Carlita Shaw, in her book, The Silent Ecocide, says that,

> *'There are about 13000 Grey Wolves left remaining in the wild, wolves are killed systematically each year in the USA, with no acknowledgement of what they can do for the ecology of wildlife reserves...their very presence increases the quality of the ecosystems as well as twenty vertebrate species thriving from their presence, they are a part of the ecosystem and when they are removed, the ecosystem suffers and biodiversity is lost. These are not subtle differences; they are vital changes when the wolf is removed from the ecology of a landscape.'21*

I sensed in my dream that the 'wolves' were also actually the shamans and the agenda was really about the extermination of indigenous systems of knowledge and ways of being. In recent years, at least fourteen shamans from the Shawi people have been murdered. Indigenous leader Alberto Pizango, president of the Interethnic Development Association of the Peruvian Rainforest (known by its Spanish acronym, AIDESEP) holds responsible both legal and illegal industries in the Amazon who poach natural resources from indigenous lands. "What is happening now in my community is organized crime," said Pizango, himself a Shawi medico who studied for seven years under a master shaman.

"This work, I would say, is done in a very subtle way by the extractive industries," Pizango said, naming the timber and oil industries as well as those involved in producing illegal drugs.

Deep ecology recognizes the importance of the inner ecosystem in relation to the outer and that change must come from within ourselves in order to effect meaningful change in the world.

> *'...the environmental crisis is a crisis of human consciousness and understanding. Our environment mirrors our state of consciousness, resulting in all current deformations and beauty...Maintaining responsibility over our internal ecology ensures a sustainable healthy external ecology.'* 22

In a way, shamans are like the wolves, their presence allows for balance and enriches the spiritual ecosystem, they are in a sense the spiritual ecologists par excellence.

CHAPTER ELEVEN

11:11, DNA AND THE RAINBOW BRIDGE

'The potent essence of creativity, the kundalini fire fused into streams of pulsating light that rippled up and down their bodies like flames in a raging burning forest, tidal waves of energy - snakes of living light. Cascading rainbows of photons swirled around and out of their heads in unimaginable radiance.' Susan Ferguson

The central thesis of Jeremy Narby's book, 'The Cosmic Serpent' is that, *'...the peoples who practice what we call 'shamanism', communicate with DNA.'* 23 During a spiritually very intense period, I realised that this was exactly what was happening to me, that my DNA was talking to me. This realisation came about when I began to experience the 11:11 phenomena. I first noticed this number code on the digital clock of my car as I was driving up the lane to my house. That night I woke up with intense kundalini flowing through me and this eventually culminated in an OBE. When I came back from the OBE I had received the following information. 11:11 means, ***Un-limited manifestation and possibility, in eternal unchanging consciousness.***

This is the most important sentence in this book; I would gladly delete everything else I have written if this could remain. It corresponds beautifully with the yogic viewpoint of the creative force of Shakti combined with the still consciousness of Shiva. 11:11 is all ones, so it is about

Oneness but also it is a communication from our DNA. Narby says of DNA that,

> *'In 4 billion years, it has multiplied itself into an incalculable number of species while remaining exactly the same.'* 24

So, DNA can also be seen as infinite manifestation and possibility in eternal unchanging consciousness. Following this I had further dreams full of numbers, which always added up to various combinations of eleven and I began to see it very frequently in waking life. The two ones in the number eleven represent the twin strands of DNA. Within the genetic code of DNA there are sixty-four possible words, which have twenty-two possible meanings. Twenty-two, is of course 11+11. In my repetitive snake dreams I sometimes encountered double-headed serpents. In one dream, whilst a black mamba chewed on my hand, a two-headed green and white striped cobra watched us. In another, I dug into the earth and pulled out a statue of a double headed serpent which when inverted became a chalice. Furthermore, in some of my dreams the snakes would be impossibly large or very small, or very small with impossibly large mouths. This also ties in with Narby's observation that, *'...DNA is a snake-shaped master of transformation that...is both extremely long and small, single and double. Just like the cosmic serpent.'* 25. During this time I had many dreams and visions of outer space, other planets and star systems. Crick, the discoverer of the structure of DNA, believed that it did not originate on Earth but arrived from outer space through panspermia, a possibility that was corroborated by my own received messages concerning our origins on this planet. In one dream I was shown a plant in a pot. Hidden in the soil were secret seeds. A voice said, *humans are seeded on this planet and this will be shown through DNA*. An African shaman showed me a cosmic egg with seeds in it. The voice said, *we are seeding across the supernova, soon we will be gone.*

Buryat shamanism holds that we have three souls; one of these contains the memory of the ancestors, the memory of our DNA. I think these cosmic dreams and visions may be the soul memory of my DNA's journey to Earth.

In the Cosmic Serpent, Narby focuses primarily on the shamanism of western Amazonia and the use of ayahuasca. His theory that these shamans are accessing information at a microscopic level was confirmed to me also in an ayahuasca ceremony. In this ceremony my consciousness was brought right down to the cellular level. I could see the cells of my body and within the cells swam numerous tiny snakes. A few months later I came across new research published in the Journal of Genetics and Genomics by Dr Ji-Long Liu's group at the Department of Physiology, Anatomy and Genetics in Oxford. They had discovered what they called 'cytoophidia' in human cells. Cytoophidium is 'cell snake' in Greek and this is exactly how they appear under the microscope.

'Cytoophidia have heads and tails and can move around. They really do look like snakes,' explains Ji-Long Liu and furthermore that, 'Amazingly, these snakes occur across the tree of life, from bugs to humans.' 26

So, by drinking a plant medicine I had clearly been shown what these scientists had discovered in their experiments, tiny serpents in our cells. It is not necessary however to ingest an entheogen to receive this information, this conversation with our DNA is a gift of the spirits to the shaman. Long before ever I had taken ayahuasca I dreamed of a ladder. I was told to climb the ladder to find the sacred tobacco. I had no idea of the intimate relationship between ayahuasca and tobacco at this time, nor of the receptors in the human brain into which a molecule of nicotine fits like a key into a lock. This effectively opens a door to certain electrical reactions, which excite the DNA. The DNA molecule looks just like a twisted ladder. My own DNA was telling me it could be 'excited' by tobacco.

The ladder is a very important symbol in many shamanic traditions as a means of ascending to the upper world. Eliade cites numerous examples. It is clear that shamans from all over the world are in conversation with DNA and that just as the mind interprets kundalini as a snake, it turns DNA into a ladder. In my dreams I would be climbing ladders, carrying ladders or be given ladders.

In a series of ayahuasca ceremonies one experience kept repeating itself, a vast crystalline structure would manifest above my head. At the same time, the sushumna would extend out of my forehead as a transparent tube, which turned upwards towards the crystal. Within this tube swam the kundalini cobra. I was very awed and a little scared of this crystalline structure and did not really understand what it was. Re-reading the Cosmic Serpent months later I was amazed to see a drawing representing consciousness as understood by the Desana of the Columbian Amazon. It shows the two hemispheres of the brain with a serpent moving through the centre towards a crystal located outside the head.

DNA itself is an aperiodic crystal, which emits photons that correspond to the spectrum of visible light and another way that DNA expresses itself to the shaman, is as the rainbow. In standard Mongolian the word *solongo* means rainbow and is related to the Dagur Mongolian word *soolong* meaning 'power dream' as the shaman travels over the rainbow in his sleep. Black Elk had visions of a flaming rainbow and Eliade notes that some Siberian drums have rainbows painted on them, the ribbons in Buryat initiations are called rainbows and that the rainbow is a bridge to the Upper World.

For me the experience of the rainbow was unforgettable. It began as a dream where I found myself looking at an ancient magical book then I looked out of the window and saw huge electrical energy in the distance. Then I looked out of another window and saw the most beautiful rainbow. It was bigger than a normal rainbow and the colours unbelievably intense and it was twisted in a double helix. I went outside to see it and realised I could fly. I said to Michèle, *we have entered the New Earth.* At this point I knew absolutely that I was in another dimension. Holding hands with Michèle we walked through a town, in front of us the rainbow transformed into the shape of a huge gothic arch. We continued under the rainbow arch, walking past some beings from another planet and came to a pillar of light. It came up from the earth with all the colours of the rainbow like a kundalini-awakened spine. Beside it, floating in the air, a silvery willow-the-wisp spirit pointed at it, as if to say, *'look at this!'* Then the rainbow took the form of a comet and rushed into my chest.

To me the Vertical Pillar of Light is our path to higher consciousness, the Rainbow Bridge and the ladders, our DNA. It is through changing this that our higher consciousness manifests and spreads in the world. Scientists are now suggesting that memory is passed on via DNA. What kind of memory are we passing on to our descendants via the blueprint of our individual DNA? Buryat shamanism holds that,

> *'The three souls reside in the spherical field of energy that envelops the physical body. This sphere has an upright axis within it, pierced by seven holes that correspond to the seven chakras. The suld soul resides at the crown of the head, where there is a direct connection to Father Heaven through the small tenger that resides there. The other two souls oscillate back and forth through the holes of the body axis in a sine-wave pattern.' 27*

The oscillation in a sine-wave pattern of the two other souls bears more than a passing resemblance to the ida and pingala nadis either side of sushumna and the double helix of DNA. The two other souls are known as the ami and the suns. The ami soul is the carrier of ancestral genetic memory, in other words the memory of the DNA of the physical body we have incarnated in. The suns soul carries the collective experiences of past lives. I suspect that the balancing of ida and pingala nadis in a kundalini awakening may also bring these two souls into balance bringing the memory of our present DNA entwined with the memory of our transmigrating soul in a double helix up the spine to the Oneness at the crown chakra.

So, DNA takes the form of a double helix and presents itself to shamans as a serpent. It is surely no coincidence that kundalini not only presents itself to the awakening person as a serpent but may also rise up the spine in a full intersecting double helix. If we consider the yogic view that we live in an illusion of separation, one soul pretending to be many we can relate this to the fact that DNA as the building block of all life, is one thing, seeming to hide itself in multiplicity. It would seem to me that the animating force and consciousness within DNA with which shamans interact to obtain knowledge is nothing less than the creative force behind the sacred illusion. Shamans are talking with kundalini Shakti. That scientists, yogis and shamans all uncover snakes within us makes me wonder if the inherent fear of snakes so many of us have is not simply a the fear of remembering our true selves.

> *'It was a wonderful time -the Time before Forgetting. One wonders if and when the approach of ensuing cycles was sensed. For inevitably and imperceptibly, the frequencies of the temporal illusory hologram changed, becoming gradually diminished and dulled. The brilliance of the seething snakes of light from the kundalini force dimmed and as consciousness*

descended further into matter, was suppressed, cloaked – choked.
The few who quite reasonably, desperately clung to what had been before were still able to see the snakes of light writhing from the heads of beings that possessed Real Power. But most could not. Most did not remember their own flames of thought, the once radiant wild spraying photon rivers, the shimmering snakes of light. And they began to be afraid.
The frequencies of fear led human consciousness further into isolation, separation, density and delusion. Cut off from the true memory of Oneness, this world descended into violence fed on the contagious miasma of fear. The Sacred Warriors of better times, whose dharma was to protect Truth, left the Earth.
As time crawled inexorably on, fear and greed became the norm. The creators, who had forgotten who they were, inserted unending wars into the astonishing hologram called Life. Thus began thousands of years of senseless, intentional, unstoppable killing -taking what others created and loved. Endless wars soaked the earth with blood and the once visible luminescent snakes of light vanished. Thus began all of written history.' 28

It is astonishing and wonderful to me that through my own journey of remembrance, the healing of my own cumha, it is revealed to me that I am indeed, at one level of my being, a shimmering snake of light. Now, when I close my eyes and turn inwards I can sometimes see a serpent dividing the hemispheres of my brain. It swims around a central vertical axis; sometimes it's double, sometimes single. When it is single it looks exactly like a design by an unknown noaide on one of the lost Sami drums.

This period concluded with a dream in which I found myself looking at an old rusty ladder. I was about to climb it when I was told, *no,* and I was presented with a brand new, shiny ladder. Much later, when the spirit of the Bear came to guide me in the making of a Sami style drum, I was to climb the silver light ladder of my own DNA, into other dimensions.

CHAPTER TWELVE
ENTHEOGENIC DREAMS

Along with the shamans and animals, came the dreams of the plants. In waking life I have only ever taken two entheogens, ayahuasca and *amanita muscaria*, but in the dream state I encounter not only these but many other plant teachers. Often I will enter into communion with the plant, which leads to an altered state of consciousness just as impressive as if taken in waking life. Although all peoples have been given there own sacred plant teachers, I sense that all these plant teachers are connected and work together in the spirit world.

In the following dream, ayahuasca made her presence felt through the jaguar.

I'm in a house doing the washing up and putting rubbish in bags, I'm having a good clean up. I go to the window and suddenly a jaguar appears, his paws on the sill. He then bounces happily around the garden. I then realise that there are other people in the house and it is a spiritual retreat. A man with fractal ayahuasca patterns on his forehead pours some seeds into my hand. I give some to Michèle saying, 'it's pergalum harmala'. The man says, 'these will keep you going in the coming months'.

The house cleaning reflected the personal cleansing I was doing in anticipation of taking Ayahuasca. Pergalum harmala is Syrian rue, a plant used as an alternative to ayahuasca in what are known as ayahuasca-analogues. It feels as if ayahuasca and Syrian rue were in co-operation here.

In my first ayahuasca retreat a famous Sufi singer from India took part in the ceremonies. In a vision I saw her kneeling in a temple, her head arched right back, the Ayahuasca vine growing out of her mouth towards the heavens. Plants that have a strong relationship or association with ayahuasca have also come.

I dream Michèle and I are smoking mapacho (jungle tobacco) from a sacred pipe. I open a cabinet; it is full of San Pedro cacti.

Ayahuasca is said to love tobacco. The San Pedro cactus, a phallic expression, is her polar masculine opposite, the Shiva to her Shakti. Although I have never taken this entheogen its spirit has nevertheless been very communicative. In a dream a shaman told me, *when the Chavin call, you must go*. Chavin de Huantar is one of the most ancient and important temple in Peru. It is set in a very remote location, high in the Andes and was designed specifically for the ritual use of San Pedro. Next I dreamed I was sat in San Pedro ceremony with a giant who told me how they had called down the Anaconda Terra to Earth from the sky. After this, in shamanic consciousness I was brought to Chavin. Two giant black centipedes came to protect me. They are the scariest spirit animals I have ever seen, no negative forces could come near me with these bodyguards and I walked freely around the temple complex. It was very beautiful and great columns of golden light connected Chavin to the Heavens.

Considering that African spirit shamans came to me it is not surprising that their great entheogen, iboga, also came in dreams.

I go into a beautiful house. Some women give me Iboga in a silver cup. I go to the top of the building. There are beautiful gothic windows. My friend that I brought for ayahuasca is there; we talk because he still needs healing. There is a narrow gothic arch in front of us with light streaming through it. He tries to go through but can't make it yet.

Mushrooms appear frequently in my dreams; they are usually glowing to get my attention, like the power animals. I have found that *amanita muscaria*, commonly known as 'fly agaric' has a great sense of humour. In a shamanic state of consciousness I found myself walking down a street pushing a wheelbarrow. The wheelbarrow was full of ceramic bowls, all spotted red and white like the mushroom. They were the type of bowls you might use for breakfast cereal, so I think the mushroom was saying, eat me. Then I came to a house, and on the doorstep was a radio, again spotted red and white, surrounding it were *amanita muscaria* mushrooms. Blasting out of the radio was a song that went, *we are the mushrooms, we are the mushrooms,* over and over! This made me laugh but I knew they wanted me to enter the house, so I did. Within the house I received important information that I needed to help another person, so there was a serious aspect to this but the way that the mushroom chose to broadcast its message via '*amanita muscaria* radio' was hilarious. I detail later on, the truly amazing dream communications from *amanita muscaria*.

Trees, herbs and flowers have also brought their messages; it is not only the entheogens that are teachers. Once, during an asthma attack, I asked for ways that might help me with this condition. First, I saw my stepdaughter cutting lavender, she gave me a sprig and told me it was good. Then I saw Michèle pointing at a wall where two plants grew. One had small bright yellow flowers and I recognised it as St. John's Wort. The other was like a small shrub with chicken eggs stuck on it. At first I couldn't figure this out but then it came to me, it was aubergine, also known as eggplant! A little research soon revealed that essential oil of lavender is very effective in relieving mild asthma attacks. Although St John's Wort is a powerful medicinal plant, it turned out that it should be avoided when taking asthma inhalants as it can cause an adverse reaction. The aubergine was interesting in that some studies have shown that asthmatics may benefit from cutting this vegetable and all other members of the nightshade family from their diet. Contrary to this, the traditional medicine of Suriname uses the roots of the plant as an asthma cure. It is amazing that such a simple presentation could provide me with so much information, yet this is how plant spirit shamanism works.

I have found the communications from trees to be very beautiful and powerful. When I returned from Peru I started to think how I could apply what I'd learned about shamanism there, into a European context. The dieting of trees made me think about the shamans and druids of ancient times in Europe, how trees were sacred to them and I had a strong intuition that they must have been doing something very similar. Not much has survived as to what they actually did as theirs was an oral tradition. It has been suggested etymologically that the word druid means ‘wisdom of the oak’. I became convinced in fact that they learnt from the plants and trees directly as do the curanderos in Peru. The oak was noted as being particularly sacred to the druids and with this in mind I decided to diet a large and beautiful oak on my land under which I often meditated. I filled a bottle with water from an ancient holy spring near my house and I put twigs and leaves from the tree in it and left it to marinate for a couple of days. I then drank the water three times a day and put oak leaves under my pillow at night. I straight -away felt very 'green'. The first night I had a beautiful dream. I found myself climbing a mountain. To get to the top I had to pass through the Tomb of Lao Tzu, there was a guardian who let me pass. I made it to the snow covered summit where there was a green plant growing. I knew I must bring some of the plant back with me for other people. I managed to grab a few stalks and leaves before sliding quickly down again. The next day I received a beautiful vision. I saw the oak tree and a lamb. They were joined as one, the lambs nose reached up to touch the tree’s branches that were leaning down to meet it. Oak in Irish is ‘daour’ meaning door and my experience confirmed that the oak is certainly a doorway into the spirit worlds.

In a vision the oak tree showed itself to me with a luminous blue khadag (Mongolian prayer scarf) tied around it. I had one of these, so I obliged and tied it around a branch, the tree looked very beautiful like this. This led to another vision where I was shown the root system of the tree. I could see into the Earth and below the roots a vast black anaconda spiralled. I could see that via this snake the Earth consumed all energy.

Above the anaconda, the tree roots drew up the recycled energy as silver light, bringing it back up and out into the world.

The Amazonian shamans say that one plant will sometimes direct them onto the medicine of another. I sense that the relationship I'd formed with *amanita muscaria* connected me to the spirit of the birch, one of the trees the mushroom lives in symbiosis with. The tree appeared to me in a dream and I woke up suddenly with the word 'birch' reverberating through my head. The following night in a vision my head was enveloped in green birch leaves. The next day I made birch leaf tea and discovered that a course of this was exactly what I needed to treat a health problem I had at the time. It is clear to me that the trees have not forgotten us and still offer their friendship and healing, if we are only open enough to remember and let them in.

In a beautiful dream full of classic enlightenment metaphors I found myself standing in a clear flowing stream. All around my feet were water lilies. Looking down I realised that the whole universe was contained within each flower. I collapsed on my knees, crying at the beauty of this, as clear water splashed on my face.

CHAPTER THIRTEEN

THE COMING OF THE TIGER

One night a Mongolian man came in a dream. He said, *I used to be a shaman, are you sure you want this?* This was my udha, the unique shamanic spirit that each shaman has that is responsible for the calling of the shaman. The fact that I'm Irish and the udha Mongolian may seem odd but as Sarangarel explains in Chosen by the Spirits,

> *'Even now new udha are being produced as the human population increases and the need for new shamans grows. Nevertheless, there are many lonely and neglected udha spirits who are seeking new partners, even if these partners may be from outside the culture in which the udha was incarnated during its lifetime as a human being.' 29*

In truth, I wasn't sure if I wanted 'this', whatever this actually was. I must confess also that I really didn't know what to do with this new drum of oak and stag. I knew that it had to be brought into the world but its secrets eluded me for many months. I loved to play it out in nature at night under the moon but it felt just like an active meditation to me. Kundalini would rise, I would have a sense of wellbeing but I was not taking a journey and I was very much aware of this. Having experienced many different states of consciousness and even spontaneous shamanic journeys on occasion I knew that something was missing. I felt confused, I even began to think that the drum wasn't for me and that I should find the right person to pass it on to. In retrospect I can see that I was actually going through a process of spiritual modification that would allow me to understand the drum when the time was right.

The most important changes centred on my chest area. This occurred in the winter, there was heavy snowfall and I was alone. The first thing that happened was that when I sat down to meditate intense pain rose up from either side of my chest, through my jawbones into my head. This was extremely scary and I thought I might be having some kind of heart attack. After much research on the Internet I couldn't find anything that matched my symptoms exactly. I suspected the pain might be spiritual but I was still rather concerned and that night I left all the doors of the house open, despite the cold, so that if I died in my sleep the animals wouldn't be trapped. Over the next couple of days I found myself compelled to take very long walks in the snow. Then, something amazing happened, I awoke sometime during the night to see a swirling mass of electric blue energy above me; it was the size of a football. It flew straight into to my third eye and I convulsed as intense energy rushed through me. There was so much energy that the hallway light switched itself on and off. The next afternoon, after lighting a big fire in the range, I once again sat down to meditate. The intense pain came on straight away but this time the blockages were broken through, the pain went and I found myself in the vast space of the heart. For a moment I wasn't in the room and thought I would pass out but eventually I came back to normal consciousness. I think this was meant to happen when I was alone, it was a special time and I continued my long walks in the snow and meditations.

Eventually on the spring equinox a transformation occurred. One day I was something like a yogi and the next day I was also something like a shaman. The night before the equinox I dreamed of a tree with deep red berries, around it, I sensed strange and wonderful paths where I felt I had journeyed before with Michèle. Then the dream became lucid, as Michèle appeared and began chanting a mantra. I then came fully conscious and saw a Mayan sun disc made of gold in my third eye. In the disc, the head of a tiger appeared, it lifted its head, roared and walked out of the disc into me. The next day someone asked me to take a journey for them, I was reluctant to try this but at the same time I felt perhaps it was sign. To my great surprise I was able to take a journey and come back with clear and accurate information. During this journey a large grey wolf came to me, beside it was a glowing ball of red fire. The next day I decided to do some drumming. I opened sacred space and began. The kundalini came strongly into my brain, it balanced exactly on both sides to bring my brain into perfect equilibrium before entering my third eye. Suddenly the spirits were there, they had their hands in the air, they were dancing joyfully as if to say, *at last he's arrived, we've been calling for so long!* Shortly after this, in meditation, a tunnel opened and the Tiger leapt through it and ran around happily. It has been with me ever since, this spirit Tiger of whom I had dreamed so often before this moment. I can't describe the joy of this meeting and the great honour it is to have such a guardian with me. Shortly after this many spirit shapes began to flow into me and I knew the Ancestors had come. I saw them lined up before me row upon row, hundreds going back in time, lives lived that I might live mine. For several months after the equinox, meditation was impossible, because as soon as I closed my eyes, the Tiger would appear and take me journeying through the cosmos. There are many different states of consciousness from our everyday waking one. Dreams, lucid dreams, astral projection and more but perhaps the least understood is the shamanic journey. Before I received the ability to journey I had in fact done things very similar on a few occasions before but simply didn't understand what it was. Once, during a period of intense kundalini a spiral appeared in my third eye and I went through it. I found myself in a lucid dream. I was naked, in a house. I found I had special abilities like opening and closing doors with my mind. Within the dream I astral projected and found myself fully aware but in a previously un-encountered state of consciousness. The colours were really bright and stunning, I was shown various things including many clocks all set to different times. This was a first shamanic lesson, that all times are happening at once. After this I an Indian woman came and spoke to me in a language I didn't understand. I told her this. She then took my hands and said, *you have done very well.*

It was really not until that equinox when the Tiger came that I really understood the shamanic journey and that I could do it at will. Siberian, Sami and other shamanic traditions have a model of the universe where there are three worlds along the central axis of the World Tree. These are the Lower, Middle and Upper worlds. The Sami called these, Ylinen (the Upper world, realm of gods and light spirits), Keskinen (the Middle World, spirit side of this mundane world) and Alinen (the

Lower world, realm of power animals and ancestral spirits). This scenario is clearly depicted on many of their drums. Rather than seeing these three worlds as being stacked one on top of the other they are really more superimposed upon each other and in constant interaction.

The Tiger would come, ask me to follow and we would travel through various tunnels and vortexes to the various worlds. I might find myself going downwards at tremendous speed to the Lower world and I would follow the Tiger as a bird, soaring high with eagles I would see it running across plains filled with reindeer or oceans full of leaping dolphins and orca. Sometimes the Tiger would take me up the tree trunk. We would climb together, then jump off and scale a cliff face, travel at high speed on a meandering river. The first time I went up the Tree, I pulled myself out onto a plateau where tribal people were waiting for me. I walked ahead and they parted before me and I came to a huge rock covered in petroglyph stick figures. I watched as the figures began to dance.

CHAPTER FOURTEEN

CELTIC KUNDALINI ON THE MUSICAL TREE

'He was a harp; all life that he had known and that was his consciousness was the strings; and the flood of music was a wind that poured against those strings and set them vibrating with memories and dreams. He did not merely feel. Sensation invested itself in form and colour and radiance, and what his imagination dared, it objectified in some sublimated and magic way. Past, present and future mingled; and he went on oscillating, across the broad, warm world...' Jack London

Behind all this intense phenomena the harp was still providing the background music. The true name for this instrument is clairseach (Irish) or clarsach (Scottish). Unlike modern neo-Celtic harps whose strings are usually nylon, the clairseach has strings made of metal, usually brass but sometimes silver and even gold. This is the harp of legend, the instrument of the gods and heroes. Its music was given by the greatest of Irish Gods, the Dagda and through the three strains of music, Goltraighe, Sauntraighe and Geantrai, it had the power to make men laugh, cry and sleep. In the old poems and stories the harps often have special powers and personalities and are a bridge between this world and other realms, a bit like a shamanic drum in other cultures. The instrument also has a deep connection to nature and was sometimes referred to as the musical tree or Crann nan Tued, the Tree of Strings.

When I got my first clairseach, a very small simple instrument based on a carving from an Irish monastery I was simply blown away by the sound and was gripped with a fervour to learn that I hadn't experienced since my teenage years. For most of my life I had been accustomed to being a musically advanced individual and enjoyed the various kudos that come with that but now I was a complete beginner again. What was in my head could not be translated to my fingers. I found myself with the ego of a great musician but with the fingers of a complete novice. This in fact was wonderful as it began to initiate the process of taking down my ego a peg or two. The approach of surrendering my musical identity to this new instrument coupled with meditative practice was very effective.

I was attracted to this harp because it spoke to something very ancient and deep within me. I felt there was a mystical music in my soul, which could not be expressed on the instruments I was playing. As I progressed I resolved to acquire a more serious instrument. There are a number of surviving harps but only three from the medieval period. Two of these are in Scotland and one in Ireland. The Irish one, known as the Trinity College Harp or the Brian Boru Harp is the oldest surviving instrument, c.14th century. It is the national emblem of Ireland and sits in a glass case in the Long Room of Trinity College Dublin where the Book of Kells is also housed. This harp resonated strongly with me and after a long process of research, my harp maker and I were allowed to examine this priceless artefact and produce an almost exact copy. Looking at the harp with my new found shamanic eyes it became clear to me that there was something astonishing encoded within the structure and decoration of this particular harp.

It is my personal view that the clairseach was originally a shamanic/spiritual instrument. The clairseach consists of four pieces of wood. A soundbox carved out of a solid block of willow and closed with a backplate, a curved forepillar and a harmonic curve. The great harper and researcher Ann Heymann has discovered that certain gender characteristics correspond to the various parts, the soundbox being feminine, the forepillar masculine and the harmonic curve, hermaphrodite. The hollowed out soundbox can be seen as the womb. The soundboard is flat, but when tensioned by the strings, the wood bellies up as if pregnant with sound. The forepillar has a phallic quality and actually penetrates the soundbox via a mortise and tenon joint. The harmonic curve which links these two together is both penetrated by the forepillar and penetrates the soundbox, hence hermaphrodite. However, when I looked at the harp a much deeper interpretation was revealed to me, that the Trinity College Harp essentially represents the process of spiritual enlightenment in the human being. For me the key to this is the forepillar. Carved on the forepillar is an animal; it could be a snake or a salmon. From a kundalini perspective either one works. There are no snakes in Ireland but there is the Salmon of Knowledge. The salmon returns to the source and therefore works well as an Irish kundalini symbol. Furthermore there are two heads, one going up and the other going down depicting the ascent of kundalini and its return back down into the individual. The motive of the ascending and descending serpent can also be found at Monasterboice on the tenth century Cross of Muiredach. Here, carved in high relief we have a panel known as Dextra Dei, the Right Hand of God.

> *'... two interlacing serpents appear one heading downward the other upward, enframing three human heads in ascending series, with a human right hand above, reaching to the centre of a crowning halo-like ornamented disc. If this is not a specific reference to the top four states of an ascent of the sushumna, the sense of such an appearance on Christian monument commemorating the crucifixion remains to be explained.' 30*

I was sure that the forepillar represented the human spine. Just like on the Cross of Muiredach there are two serpent heads ascending and descending. On the cross the ascending head is going towards an ornamented disk symbolising enlightenment. On the harp the ascending head is moving towards a decorative mounting on the front of the harmonic curve. This contains mountings for two large crystal cabochons. The lower one is missing but the casing for it is eye shaped. The one above is a clear crystal. So here we have the kundalini serpent on the spine heading up to the third eye and union at the crown. The descending head representing the return of these united energies into the individual. It then made sense to me that the harmonic curve represented the unification of divine male and female energies. Contrary to mainstream European practice, the Gaelic harp was always played on the left shoulder with the feminine left hand playing the treble and the masculine right hand, the bass. This theme of male and female continues in the strings, as the trebles were considered feminine and the bass masculine. This is further reinforced by the presence of two strings called na comhluighe. These are two strings tuned to the same pitch, symbolically dividing the scale. In Gaelic, comhluighe means, 'lying together'. Divine male and female strings lying together; separate yet resonating the same frequency. The original harp was painted and traces still remain, the colours are red and blue. In Buryat shamanism the centre of consciousness of the human being is seen as a star of red light in the chest and the direct connection to the divine as a blue star at the crown of the head. In my own meditations these have been the two colours that have come the most and they are of a depth and quality beyond anything that can be experienced in ordinary reality.

The entire harp is intricately decorated with wood-burning and carving. Of particular interest are the roundels containing various animals including wolf-dogs and wild boar. There is also a lion fighting a dragon, a metaphor not dis-similar, to a jaguar fighting an anaconda. These may represent spirit or power animals. Hints of this and a shamanic state of consciousness can be found in the ancient tales.

> *'While they were at Cruachan, Ailill asked Fraoch if the harpers would play after dinner. This was the condition of these harps. There were harp-bags (crotbuilcc) of the skins of otters about them, ornamented with coral, (Partaing) with an ornamentation of gold and of silver over that, lined inside with snow-white roebuck skins; and*

these again overlaid with black-gray strips of skin; and linen cloths, as white as the swan's coat, wrapped around the strings. Harps (Crota) of gold, and silver, and Findruine, with figures of serpents, and birds, and greyhounds upon them. These figures were made of gold and of silver. Accordingly as the strings vibrated these figures ran around the men. They [the harpers] played for them then, until twelve men of Ailill's and Medb's household died of crying and emotion.'31

The way these figures come 'off' the harps bears a striking similarity to what may happen in shamanic drumming in the Sami tradition.

'One of the original and oldest names for the Sami shaman drum is govadas. It means an instrument that emanates images. The unique thing was thus the view that there were images coming out of them when they were used in the right way.' 32

The harp is also covered in many mysterious shapes and symbols including concentric circles like those found in sites like Newgrange. The patterns on the left side of the harmonic curve feel particularly archaic and have yet to be satisfactorily interpreted. I speculate that they may have been used for purposes of divination and I envision the shaman harper in a state of trance moving his tuning key over the symbols in the same way that a Sami noaide moved a pointer over the symbols on his drum.

I speculated on the comhluighe and how perhaps they were used shamanically on the harp. Sound and rhythm are often used in shamanism to induce and maintain an altered state of consciousness. The most common instrument used for this is the drum. One hundred and eighty beats per minute will induce a theta brainwave state, conducive to entering a shamanic state of consciousness. It is not only the repetitive beat that contributes to this state but also the complex harmonics generated by the drum. Perhaps, the harp was played alongside a drum for this purpose. In Ireland there is a traditional frame-drum, the bodhrán. Today, it is used exclusively as a musical instrument with very complex playing techniques having evolved to provide rhythmic accompaniment to Irish traditional music. I sense strongly though, that it is a vestige of an Irish shamanic drum. The bodhrán has a round wooden frame, with an animal skin, usually goat, stretched over it, just like most shamanic drums. At the back, the wooden hoop is braced with two pieces of wood in a cross pattern. This is reminiscent not only of the 'four directions' but also of the interior of some Siberian sacred drums. In Siberia, the vertical part of this basic handle is sometimes developed into a spirit figure, and the horizontal part used to hang various magical objects. Furthermore, the earliest bodhráns were sometimes called tambourines as, just like Siberian drums, they had jingles attached to them, to create additional sounds. That the bodhrán may have a shamanic origin is also suggested by the fact that it was never much used in Irish traditional music until comparatively recently, it was really due to the work of the composer Sean O'Riada, in the 1950's and 60's, that it entered popular culture as a musical instrument. The original use of the bodhrán in fact was ritualistic with strong associations with the ritual of 'Hunting the Wren' on St Stephen's Day. In Ireland, the tiny wren became the king of all birds after hitching a ride on the back of the eagle and from there flying higher even than the eagle itself.

I discovered that by playing the comhluighe rapidly and alternately it was possible to replicate the effect of the drum and its harmonics. Whilst pondering further how an Irish shaman harper might have used the instrument I remembered that there is still one great shamanic tradition that still uses a harp as its main instrument and that is Bitwi. Bitwi is a shamanic religion, which centres around one of the most powerful entheogens in the world, iboga. During the ceremony the effects of the iboga are enhanced by rapid and repetitive rhythmic motifs played on the harp accompanied by percussion. I suggest that the clairseach and the bodhrán may have also been used together in this manner.

I was delighted to find that in Gabon the harp is imbued with a deep spiritual symbolism uncannily similar to what I was seeing in my harp. What I found was that,

> *'the soundbox of the harp, covered with antelope skin is seen as symbolic of the stomach of the female principle...there are two basic colours red female and white male painted on either side of the soundbox representing sexual union...the support arm represents male potency and also the backbone..the conjunction of support arm and*

> *soundbox, backbone and stomach all express sexual union.' 33*

Regarding the strings,

> *'...the four chords of the highest pitch are feminine, the four lowest masculine...as the harp is played masculine and feminine tones intermingle in another expression of that union which is the source of all vitality.' 34*

This spiritual aspect of the harp expressed itself also in my dreams. A common theme was the harp as kundalini. Several times the serpent would slither off the forepillar of the harp, rear up and talk to me. On another occasion I saw an old man sitting by a fulacht fia, an ancient Irish cooking pit. The snake of the harp was on the ground slithering towards him. In one breathtakingly beautiful dream the harp revealed itself as a portal and connection to other worlds. In the dream I saw my mother. From her hands she spun a golden harp string. It extended out in front of her and passed through the frame of the harp. The harp frame was like a window and as my eyes followed the golden string through it I could see a beautiful landscape of rolling hills, trees and temples. Sitting just inside this other world was a statue, half woman, and half snake. She turned her face towards me.

Eventually, the third part of the Peruvian trinity came to me, I dreamed of a condor. In the dream I saw a little girl, she transformed into a condor, flew right up to my face, spread her wings and froze like this in mid-air. I woke with a start and knew immediately I had been gifted some music. I went to the harp and played straight away my first spirit song. It was fully formed, no compositional process, a gift. It was the first of several pieces of music given to me in altered states of consciousness to be expressed on the harp. I called it Irish Icaro. A friend of mine Barbara Karlik, uses her clairseach to journey and in a vision, saw her clairseach within a tree. To me the harp as the Tree of Strings can be seen as a musical expression of the Tree of Life, an extension of the kundalini awakened spine, a conduit for higher consciousness vibrating out into the Sacred Illusion.

CHAPTER FIFTEEN
THE ANACONDA AND THE COBRA

Over time it felt like the spirits were constantly working on me. Many times I would see them sitting in ceremonies in front of me. They would reach into my third eye or put or throw things into me. There was quite a stressful time when my mother-in-law was dying. She faded gradually over about a year. I had many dreams about her and felt strongly that I was to assist in her passing in some way. In the days before her passing the spirits began to show me a new place, impossible to describe, not focused like the tunnel, more of a vast shimmering that would open wide to reveal another dimension. The first time I experienced this I saw the shimmering and a thick spiral appeared within it. Out of the spiral came an anaconda followed by an angel. The angel opened a portal and I could see another world, the angel beckoned me but I was too tired to follow. On the day she died I was in another country. I knew her time was coming and I lay on the bed and prayed for her. Again the shimmering space opened up and a spirit reached out and pulled me in. Here I could see my mother in law in the bed of her hospital. She got out of bed and sat in a chair. Two spirits were with her. They performed some actions then threw her spirit out of her body. She flew upwards and was gone.

Following this I returned to Ireland for her funeral. One night while staying in the house, sleeping in that same room where Spirit had first entered into me I had another extraordinary experience. It began as a dream. In the dream I was in a house and I 'knew' a giant anaconda was outside. I was scared and as usual worried about my cats, so I made sure all the doors and windows were locked. Once I was sure everyone was safe I decided to peak out the door to see the anaconda. I opened the door a crack and could see a yard. On the far side was a huge barn. By the barn reared up to the same height as the barn roof was a snake, not an anaconda but the kundalini cobra. This was such a shock that I came to full consciousness. At this point a spiral appeared in front of me and from it emerged the anaconda. The anaconda then 'swam' into my forehead through my brain and out of my crown chakra. This was an incredible sensation and for a long time after I felt like there was a tunnel about the thickness of a mans arm, running through my head.

There are in fact parallels to this experience in both yoga and shamanism. In kundalini yoga there is a meditation called Kirtan Kriya. Part of this involves envisioning the syllables of the mantra, SA TA NA MA, entering via the crown chakra, passing through the brain and exiting at the third eye. This is said to stimulate what they call the ‘golden cord’, which is the connection between the pineal and pituitary glands. This golden cord is certainly the pathway taken by my anaconda. The shamans of the Desana, in the Amazon say, that dividing the two hemispheres of the brain is a fissure and in this fissure swims an anaconda. Sometimes it is said that two snakes, an anaconda and a rainbow boa are entwined in this fissure.

A year or so after this experience, Michèle was painting the picture that would become the cover of this book. It shows the very powerful image of a stunningly patterned constrictor moving over a shamanic drum. The act of painting induced for her, a visionary dream that closely mirrored my experience. In the dream she was walking on a path through the jungle, on one side were trees and on the other a lake of clear water. She became aware that in the trees a vast constrictor with beautiful markings was watching her. Then out of the water emerged a giant coral snake, which reared up and began to bite her. The coral snake is highly venomous and I discovered it is from the family *elapidae*, the same as the cobra! I was amazed at the corroboration of the imagery in our two experiences and how it works on multiple levels. In one sense these two serpents are certainly DNA. The path Michèle was on can also be seen as the sushumna and the serpents either side, as ida and pingala nadis. The polarities of lunar and solar, here become, constriction and venom. The two snakes can also be seen as the different aspects of Shakti. The constrictor being the aspect that binds us with its coils in the illusion, the coral snake emerging from the waters of pure consciousness, the aspect that reveals the illusion, through the transformative 'death' induced by its venom. Two serpents, that actually are one.

In a vision I saw Michèle, standing alone in a forest. In her hands she was holding up the huge skull of an anaconda. It was gleaming white in the darkness with very impressive teeth. She said, *the anaconda must be fed at every full moon,* meaning to me, that at those times I must honour my shamanic spirits. Personally, I see the anaconda and the cobra as the two strands of awakening, twin serpents of shamanism and yoga, entwined within me.

CHAPTER SIXTEEN
THE GOD IN THE GRASSHOPPER

'Those who see all creatures in themselves
And themselves in all creatures know no fear.
Those who see all creatures in themselves
And themselves in all creatures know no grief.
How can the multiplicity of life,
Delude the one who sees its unity.'
The Isha Upanishad

Although the presence of such spectacular spirit animals as anacondas and bears, cobras and tigers was wonderful, some of my most beautiful experiences were with the smaller beings like molluscs and insects. At one point I had a succession of dreams. In the first I was standing in a room with a large window. The window was covered in bees. I opened the window to let the bees out; there was a beautiful garden outside. Once the bees had flown out I could see a single small snail stuck to the window. In another dream I was cycling across a bridge. I stopped and saw a lake, lush vegetation and swans. Something on the ground caught my eye so I bent and picked it up. I found I was holding a tiny statue of a snail. The snail is hermaphrodite, symbolising the union of opposites, its shell a microcosmic spiralling reflection of the universe. When I was very young my mother would read me stories and one of my favourites was about a little snail. The little snail lives in the rhubarb patch and is warned by his mummy not to wander off alone but of course he heads off on an adventure and gets lost. Eventually he discovers the snail trail he has left and finds his way back. This is a wonderful metaphor of how we ourselves discover our spiritual way home after being lost. Despite hearing this story over and over again, my five-year old mind never failed to be gripped by the tension of the narrative and the joy of the little snails return home. Perhaps it is like this for the Oneness, pure joy, as slowly but surely we spiritual snails find our way home to the divine rhubarb patch.

This period concluded with one of the most awe-inspiring enlightenment moments of my entire journey. I dreamed I was in an old stone building. In front of me was a huge gothic archway. Through the arch I could see a beautiful garden. Hanging from the sky, framed in the exact centre of the arch was a single strand of spider silk. I watched as a green grasshopper flew down from the left and landed on it. At this point I was looking at the grasshopper from the side. The grasshopper then turned to face me and spread out its arms. It grew to fill the whole space of the arch and morphed into a fractal grasshopper, each side mirroring the other exactly. The fractal patterns were gorgeous, in various stunning shades of green. It had fingers that extended into long green tendrils that connected to everything in the garden and the universe beyond. It stayed like this, looking at me for a few moments before blowing away in the wind on the strand of spider silk. I felt the connection of everything in nature, that it was the same thing looking out of every eye. The God in the Grasshopper, my mind was blown.

CHAPTER SEVENTEEN

SHAPESHIFTING

Shapeshifting is a peculiarly shamanic and little understood phenomena. In my experience it manifests in different ways. It is possible for your consciousness to shape-shift into an animal in dream and journey states with various degrees of intensity. Once I found myself in the jungle with a curandero. He sat on my chest and blew tobacco smoke on me. My consciousness immediately shape-shifted into a mouse. Mouse-me ran into a mouse hole in the earth. In the hole I experienced exactly what it was like to be a mouse. The little hole was vast, like a cathedral to me and the other denizens of the earth like spiders and centipedes were uncomfortably large. Eventually my consciousness couldn't hold the shift anymore and I came back to my human size, bursting out through the earth to the surface. The size difference aside, I felt there was very little difference between being a man or a mouse.

A more intense form of shapeshifting came when I was receiving initiatory experiences from the polar bear. Being attacked by an animal in a dream is a typical form of shamanic initiation and to this end the polar bear returned. I dreamed of being in a sea between Ireland and the Nordic lands. Whales were with me, teaching me to slow my heart rate and hold my breath to dive deep into this cold northern ocean of spirit. Then, a giant polar bear appeared, grabbed my arm and began to savage me and shake me like a rag. The polar bear then stood up and walked like a man into a clear icy sea. I was then pulled out of my body, the polar bear was standing waist-deep in water, its paws raised in the air. From between its legs a dark haired spirit child swam towards me. That the polar bear should be an initiatory animal for me did seem unusual as it predominantly associated with Inuit shamanism. However, I discovered that polar bears trace their family tree back to Ireland. Genetic evidence shows they are descended from brown bears living in Ireland during the last Ice Age. Scientists extracted mitochondrial DNA from the teeth and bones of seventeen bears found at eight cave sites across Ireland. Ten Irish brown bears from the ice age period between ten thousand and thirty-eight thousand years ago had the maternal DNA that is now seen in every polar bear. So, in this sense, the polar bear is a perfect animal to initiate an Irish shaman.

That night a profoundly beautiful gift was given; the spirit Tiger took full possession of me. It was in a way similar to that time in Ireland all those years before. I awoke in the early hours and the Tiger entered me from the left hand side and again I felt thick viscous spirit energy. I was taken completely control of, the part that was 'me' in my body was very, very small, one percent, ninety-nine percent was Tiger. I was full of delicious spirit ecstasy, a sort of ‘wild’ kundalini, my spine was alight my whole body electrified. My hands became claws and I was growling. Although my physical body was still human, my spiritual body had shapeshifted into a Tiger. After this the Tiger energy remained with me and I received a profound healing on both the emotional and physical level. Emotional and health issues that had been troubling me vanished and I walked with the strength of the Tiger within me into a new life and way of being in the world.

The next night I awoke to see a tree in my third eye. It was a 'dark tree' glowing with dark light. The tree came towards me and I felt it enter into me. This time I internally shapeshifted into a tree, a different energy to the Tiger, softer and more sexual. I just lay there with the tree energy inside me. All through this I received a message, it was non-verbal, it didn't even form words in my head. It was of the importance of always doing the right thing. I think perhaps that the druids may have specialised in communing with tree spirits in this way.

The Buryat shamans call states like these, ongon orood, which means 'embodying the shamanic spirits' and may induce it at will. There was a time, when Michèle had a sore back, so I gave her a massage. During this I felt spirit energy enter into me, I heard a voice say, *THIS, is a jaguar walk*, and suddenly there was the jaguar, leaping through my third eye. I knew felt the jaguar come into me and I concentrated on letting the spirit do the healing. The jaguar is of course associated with ayahuasca and it was the great purgative power of the plant that came through because Michèle then began to feel sick and spent the rest of the night on the toilets! This is the difference between shamanic healing and other spiritual healing modalities like Reiki for example. A Reiki practitioner channels chi, universal energy, Reiki in fact means, 'high chi'. With shamanic healing, the shaman embodies the shamanic spirits and they do the healing. As Michèle's case shows, the shamanic healing goes very deep, the bad back was only symptomatic of something else entirely, needing to be released. Western medicine often tastes nice initially, but may only masks the symptoms, shamanic medicine may be bitter and unpleasant initially but can dig down to the root cause of the sickness and expel it.

I'm quite sure that truly powerful shaman can take shapeshifting much further than what I have experienced. The Buryat shaman Sarangerel said,

> *'Sometimes when you merge with animal spirits you will transform yourself into those animals-I have seen my teacher turn into a wolf and I myself have left wolf tracks in the snow!' 35*

I feel that these shapeshifting experiences were a direct result of healing my cumha, I no longer had a sense of separation, the barriers between myself, the spirits, nature and ultimately the One Soul had been broken down. I felt a certain fluidity in my spirit, that I was no longer strictly confined to regarding myself as only a human being.

One night, I saw a standing stone in a field. My Sami drum appeared and entered into it. The drum began to play, it was beating both within the stone and upon it. I felt myself merge with the stone and the drum. I was, at the one time, inside and outside the stone. I was the stone, the drummer and the drum. I was the vibration, the sound and the listener. I was the observer and the observed. I was, in essence, everything.

CHAPTER EIGHTEEN

CROW RATTLE

I walk into a room, a jaguar is in front of me pressing his third eye to the floor, he looks up as I approach. Standing by the jaguar, I find I am cradling a huge crow in my arms. The crow then sits up, places its forehead on mine, the beak pressed so hard against my nose I fear it might break. Our third eyes merge and I receive Crow medicine.

My conversation with the universe continued to intensify and one night I dreamed of a rattle. In the dream, I dug up with my hands, a red rattle from the soil, under the oak tree where I meditate. It was clear to me that this rattle wanted to be made. I began to gather the parts but did not make it straight away as I sensed something was missing. A few months later I returned from a music tour and went to sit under the oak where I hadn't been for a couple of weeks. There, in the centre of the worn patch of grass where I sit to meditate, was a pristine Jay feather. This, I knew, was for the rattle. The next day I returned to meditate and this time in exactly the same spot was a pristine crow flight feather. I was delighted and sat down and meditated with this gift, which I sensed was also for the rattle. When I got up, I took just two steps and found another, so now I had a matching pair. Following this I went for a walk with Dougal in the woods about a mile away and found a third identical crow flight feather! All these feathers seemed to begin an initiation into the element of air and in my dreams great winds would blow around me.

About a week after I sat under the oak and began to carve my rattle handle from a piece of evergreen oak I had found at the foot of the Cathar castle of Peyrepertuse. That night there was to be a super-moon and I returned later to the tree to put out some crystals for cleansing. I had a feeling as I approached the tree that something was there for me. I looked down and once again a pristine crow feather, this time a covert, perfect for tying to a rattle! A few days later I went to meditate in the woods. During the meditation I saw the spirit of a crow and a 'real' crow came and sat very close, cawing incessantly. When I returned to my house, placed on the doorstep of the kitchen was a fourth crow flight feather, so now I had two matching pairs. In a dream I found myself walking with two crow flight feathers in my hand and shapeshifting into a crow-man. That night I dreamed of standing in our field as huge winds gusted around me. Although there have clearly been some spectacular phenomena associated with my journey the result has been to make me aware that divine communication is constant and that Crow reminds to look everywhere for the magic.

Two days in a row I found a dragonfly trapped in my workshop. The door was open but each time they were reluctant to leave. They were huge, six inches long and stunning emerald green. They reminded me of a dream from years before where I had caught a turtle in a lake using a fishing rod made from a dragonfly. The dragonfly is all about transformation. I helped these emerald beauties out through the door with greatest care. I hope the same will be done for me some day. Outside I stood, with my arms raised to the sky and gave thanks. Above me in the circle of blue sky visible through the trees, a hawk appeared and spiralled above me.

The next day, as I was meditating outside, I went very deep, but eventually was drawn back by a repetitive knocking. I opened my eyes to see a woodpecker in the tree in front of me. His red tail feathers like the kundalini Shakti, his beak tapping on the tree like a shamanic drum. I walked with Dougal, I found some exquisite down feathers. I walked on and pondered the manifestation of shamanic tools into the world; a crow flight feather was in front of me on the path.

In a powerful dream experience I saw a feather floating down to earth. Then I saw a chair in a field. There were metal wires sticking out of it on which pieces of meat had been speared. They had been placed there as offerings to the huge raptor that was spiralling overhead. I went and sat in the chair and held up some meat for the raptor, which came and landed on the back of the chair. I was scared and I kept my head down, afraid to look at it. I eventually walked away and then turned back to look. As I did the raptor turned towards me and spread out its great wings. I felt I was being told to keep feeding higher consciousness, keep making offerings to Spirit. Curiously that night Michèle also dreamed of raptor feathers falling from the sky in front of her. At the new moon I again saw the tree and was filled with spiritual energy, I heard wolves howling three times in my head.

I eventually found the time to finish the rattle and decided to bury it under the oak tree and re-enact the dream of digging it up. Again there was a super-moon and I decided this was a perfect time to do it. On the day however there was a lot of tension and conflict around me and I was reluctant to do the ceremony with this kind of energy. That morning I decided to do some gardening and whilst clearing a patch I found another crow feather. Later in the afternoon as I was still pondering what to do, two crows flew close by me talking to each other. As the evening drew on I decided to take Dougal for a walk. As we approached the oak tree I said half jokingly to myself, *OK universe, if there is a feather under the tree I'll do the ceremony*. When I got there I couldn't believe that there was indeed a feather. Again Crow, and in such pristine condition it must have fallen only minutes before. So, that was decided and that evening I buried the rattle under the oak tree praying that it would absorb the knowledge of the underworld, become a link between heaven and earth and a conduit for healing in this one. The day after was the final super-moon of the series and I went at sunset and performed a ceremony for the rebirth of the rattle. I thanked the deers that had given the rattle head and the sinew, I thanked the Crow and the Jay for the feathers, I thanked the tree for the handle, I thanked the stones, seeds and crystals I had placed inside. Then, I began a journey to meet with the spirit of the rattle. As usual the Tiger came and off we went. I began to see flowers and the bees, at first I wondered why, then I remembered the beeswax on the handle and realised I'd forgotten to thank them, so I apologised and thanked them profusely. Eventually the rattle spirit flew down, my wild self came to the fore, I bared my teeth, I hissed like a snake. When I opened my eyes the silver moon was fully risen above me.

CHAPTER NINETEEN
SONG OF THE REINDEER

Towards Samhain I finally felt it was time to birth a Siberian drum that had been calling to be born for many months. It first came in a dream where I saw horses riding across a vast northern plain with coloured ribbons streaming from them in the wind. As I was waking up from the dream I could hear the tinkling of little bells. I sensed this was a drum communication, as in Siberia the drum is sometimes called the horse, which the shaman rides into the spirit world. In subsequent dreams I would find myself in beautiful lands I knew to be Siberia and where I felt great happiness. In one dream I found myself travelling in Siberia where I met a female shaman with a huge eye and wild black hair. I told her I was going to make a drum and she replied, *you mean like this one?,* and gestured to a horse. The horse had pink, white and blue ribbons on it. So I knew that the drum needed these. Some research into Siberian drum tradition revealed that the shamans use little bells called tiger bells with tiger faces on them. So I knew my drum must have these as well as the ribbons. The shamanic traditions of the far north are very closely related to the reindeer and so I acquired such a skin from Finland to make the drum. I also got a wonderfully un-round hoop, which I was delighted with as many of the older drums I saw were beautifully distorted and I loved the character this gave. The hoop, by chance, was made of beech. This was significant as this is one of the trees that *amanita muscaria*, the entheogen most associated with northern shamanic traditions, lives in symbiosis with. Although laced drums, similar to the Native American style of my first drum exist in Siberia I was shown in a journey that this was to be a drum where the skin was to be stitched to the rim. In the lacing style drum, a cross-shaped handle is formed from the lacing itself. With the stitched drum this is not possible so in Siberia handles come in several different kinds. I chose a wooden one, as this is sometimes called the 'tiger'. In Siberia the Tiger is considered the most sacred animal and I loved the association of this, the tiger bells and my own spirit tiger. For the handle I chose elder wood. This would not be a traditional choice in Siberia but I chose it for a number of reasons. Firstly, I have a long relationship with this tree as for many years I had been making reeds out of it for my uilleann pipes. This was virtually a lost art and was in a way my first shamanic expression. I took joy in producing music from the hedgerow, rather than using cane as most people did. I got to know all the elder trees in the vicinity. The elder could be harvested dead from the ground but if looking for a piece from a living tree it could only be taken when the sap was down in the roots. The lore was that the best time to do this was after the first frost after the first full moon in November. The tree was also to be asked permission and thanked otherwise bad luck would befall. This was clearly a vestige of Irish shamanic practice. Another reason for choosing elder is that in folklore it is closely associated with witches and the supernatural. It's one of the trees in the ogham alphabet and is veritable pharmacological treasure for healing. Furthermore, the elder branch has pith up its centre, which can be hollowed out. The handle of Siberian drums is also associated with the spine and I felt that the hollow elder beautifully represented the sushumna through which kundalini travels. I chose a piece with lovely blue and red markings shooting up from the bottom to symbolise this. Some Siberian drums have a twisted copper or iron wire running horizontally across the drum from which various objects of significance to the shaman could be hung. I chose for this a silver harp string to bring another touch of Ireland into the drum. Another feature of these Siberian drums is that the handle sometimes doubles into a spirit fetish called an ongon. Usually a simple spirit face is fixed to the handle and then clothes and decorations added also. I had really no idea what the spirit would look like so I asked if it might show itself to me. What came were large feline eyes, they came several times so I felt sure. I thought in fact that this might be my spirit Tiger asking to be shown. I went to the workshop and began to make the piece. It sort of unfolded naturally without any real plan or design. What emerged was certainly feline but looked more like a domestic or small wildcat than a tiger. Once I had the hoop, handle and ongon face prepared, I was ready to make the drum the next day. That night I dreamed I was in annoying petty situations and eventually found myself walking in a run down depressing housing estate in London. Just as I was wondering how I'd ended up in a place like this a bird flew up to me. It was ethereal and the most gorgeous pastel pink and blue colours. It flew right up to my face and alongside me as I walked. I said, *you must be the most beautiful bird in the universe!* I could feel its feathers fluttering on my face as I woke up, I knew it was a true spirit bird and that its colours were the same as the ribbons on the drum. I felt blissfully happy and felt my work was blessed. I got up at dawn the next morning and lowered the reindeer skin into the well to soak for several hours. I retrieved it that afternoon and spent the rest of the day stitching the drum, finishing the last stitch under the stars. I stood under the oak tree, held the drum up to the night sky and dedicated it to the service of the universe. This was just the first stage as the drum was still to be dressed and decorated and a beater made. That night I slept with the drum in my room and the magic began to happen. First the bird came again. Then the drum would rush up to my face and initiate strong dream images. I found myself in a small cave in a cliff face; the ocean was gently lapping at the entrance where I sat. Floating in the ocean were several large and very beautiful shells, like giant sea snails or nautilus. They were white and spiralled with stunning colours inside, as if each contained a universe. I was told they were called *rhino...(?)* and I had to extract something from them. I got one into the cave and out of it burst a ferocious black cat, I realised that this was the spirit of the drum. The next day I discovered that these snails actually exist, *rhinocerous vasum*, the rhinoceros vase snail! It seems the spirit of the cat was drawn up from the ocean of consciousness through the cosmic spiral of the shell. Furthermore, when examining my drum in the light I discovered that a feline face had appeared on the inside of the drum-skin just to the left of the cat face I had made. I painted the face black. The following days brought more strange dreams. In one, an old Siberian shaman with a drum appeared twice to me and supervised me cutting a skin for a truly enormous drum. In a vision I heard the word 'bluebirds'. I saw two bluebirds; many orbs of white light emerged from them and snaked of into a starry cosmos in parallel lines. I sensed they were the illuminated markings on the back of a spirit anaconda. Driving home with Michèle from the market, a small hawk flew to the left, then a huge buzzard straight ahead. When I awakened the drum in ceremony I saw the reindeer running and incredible sounds of wind and roaring emanated from the drum. That night in my dreams I found myself with the drum. I was pressing on the skin with my finger, which had a red earthy paint on it. As I pressed the skin, the face of an old medicine man began to appear, it seemed that rather than painting this face I was actually revealing what was already there. In my dream the next night I found myself in space holding a drum out in front of me. From around a corner in space came the beautiful orange red golden light of a sunrise. The light snaked in thick tendrils towards the drum. It passed through the skin and was focused and amplified before passing into me, infusing me with radiance.

CHAPTER TWENTY

DEMONIC DIVERSIONS

> *'They (shamans) are pre-eminently the anti-demonic champions; they combat not only demons and disease, but also the black magicians.'* Eliade

Newly kundalini-awakened people are actually very vulnerable to spiritual predation from human fake gurus and teachers. Some people have the perception of the kundalini-awakened person as an all knowing enlightened being but in fact more often than not they may be confused and scared. Following the huge light vision I saw in my field, I felt out of my depth and contacted someone who ran a kundalini yahoo group on the Internet. He seemed sincere, what he said to me seemed to make sense and I became active in the group. Over time, I became quite in awe of this man, as did many others. He came across as honest and caring through the Internet. Looking back, there were a lot of telltale signs that I should have spotted or perhaps was aware of but didn't want to accept, because being part of this group, I felt special, a point of view he actively encouraged. His speciality was shaktipat. This is a long established tradition in India whereby a person that has the ability to do so, awakens the kundalini of another. This is not without its problems as it can create a dependency on the part of the aspirant to the guru. This teacher would give shaktipat over the Internet several times a year. One of these shaktipats coincided with a powerful spiritual experience that happened to me and I thought that although I hadn't asked for the shaktipat I had somehow received it. The teacher was more than happy to encourage this perception, although in fact it had nothing to do with him. So, from then on I effectively gave my power to this man and felt my spiritual progress depended on his programme. Eventually this teacher who was American, was invited to Ireland to give a weekend workshop with shaktipat. Michèle and I decide to attend. I was still in awe of him but Michèle immediately began to see through him. Over the weekend he proceeded to use various subtle techniques of mind control and hypnotism much favoured by successful cult leaders. Some people might be made to feel special, others excluded. Pseudo-tantric exercises were given to create jealousy and sexual tension. He made it clear that he was all-powerful and that only he could bring us to the enlightened state. He said he could see kundalini and would awaken mine but I was already awakened and knew this. He was simply trying to put doubt in my mind to give himself more control. In fact whilst telling me I wasn't kundalini awakened, he was also telling people that clearly weren't that they were. On the night before the shaktipat I had a warning dream. In the dream I saw the teacher. He said, *do not come into my church, it is a church within a church within a church...within...within.* He carried on speaking in languages I didn't understand before reiterating again at the end, *do NOT come into my church.* I was disturbed by this but had been looking forward to the weekend so much I didn't want to listen. On the last day he took us aside and said that he was forming a community and would like us (because we were special) to be part of it. He said in 2012 the world would go to Hell but that Shakti herself had directed him to a safe place. She also had told him it was fine to have guns! I think at this point I was starting to see through him but it was Michèle that really snapped me out of it, telling me exactly what she thought of him and his whole setup. Initially I was very resentful towards Michèle for this but then suddenly the light of reason dawned and I saw clearly. Michèle had set me free. We wrote to some of the other group members to warn them, some listened, some didn't. A couple of months later, numerous accusations emerged of sexual abuse of his female students and his little empire collapsed. What was most upsetting was that the people in our small group in Ireland were all extremely vulnerable in various ways. There were people with psychological problems, others were deep in grief, some had attempted suicide, others were sincere seekers trying to free themselves from a lifetime of catholic guilt and indoctrination. They came with open hearts and open wallets into the lair of a predator. They were also some of the loveliest people that I have ever met.

I am actually very grateful for this whole episode, I met some wonderful people and learned some valuable lessons. After this I was able to interpret warning dreams that came and also recognise if I was under spiritual attack or talking to someone who didn't have my best interests at heart. At one point a friend of mine was involved with a Thai girl. This was really a money making scam, she was bleeding him dry whilst cheating on him with other men to whom she was doing the same. I actually quite liked her, it just was what it was, but she knew, that I knew what she was up to. She was from the north of the country near the Laos border. In Laos they are very big into black magic and all spells of this kind are written in Khmer script. The Thai girls go across to Laos if they want to curse someone. Through a dream I realised that she was definitely sending bad intention my way. In the dream I was walking down a street with the girl. In the middle of the road was a beautiful python. The girl went over and began to violently kick and punch the snake, then she picked it up by its neck and dragged it forcefully up and down. I was very shocked by this, not only was I dismayed at her treatment of the snake but I also sensed that what she was doing was very dangerous. After her attack on the snake (which I saw as my kundalini) she turned her back to it and couldn't see it rising up behind her. Leaves grew from its body and I watched in terror as it rose to be hundreds of feet tall, a giant python tree, looming up behind her. She never saw it but proceeded to a school building. I followed her and we entered the canteen. Here she furtively gathered as much food as she could, eating and stuffing it into her pockets at the same time. There was a desperation there and I realised that she was really still a little girl not knowing where the next mouthful of food was coming from and that this explained her behaviour in adult life. The next day I dreamed I was in a zoo standing in front of two glass cases. The sign on the top one said Reticulated Python and inside, a python was curled up contentedly. The bottom one had a sign saying Anaconda but the anaconda was missing and in its place I could see myself lying on a bed. The next day the girl told my friend that she had had a very frightening dream, a giant snake had come to see her, it wanted her to go with it, it wanted to talk to her and show her something. She was too afraid and wouldn't go. I certainly did not send this snake but it does seem that the spirit anaconda may have taken matters into its own hands! Later I think she tried again. I found myself in an altered state of consciousness sitting on my drum with a black and white striped cobra. I have never killed a snake in any spiritual situation except this one; I just knew that this cobra had to die. I crushed its head violently and threw it off the drum. The next day I did some research that confirmed to me where it had come from. There is only one species of black and white cobra and that is *naja siamensis*, the Thai spitting cobra!

Sometimes I sense that perhaps the universe is testing me by bringing me into contact with what I call 'demonic' people. I don't mean they are walking around with horns or worshipping Satan or anything like that. Often they are actually quite nice in their own way, but I recognise something subtle working through them, which they may not even be aware of themselves. Always these people seek me out. That 'subtle thing' working through them seems to be the opposite of light creative energy. It is the heavy force that wants to slow things down, to stop creative forward movement, to derail you from your spiritual path. The first of these I met at an ayahuasca retreat. We had been there two days and there was a nice ambience in the group, a good energy. Then, a couple arrived late and the energy changed immediately. I came out of my room onto the terrace where people would sit and talk and that is how I first met the woman. She was the only person there and she called me over. I sat down, introduced myself and we started talking, or rather I started talking. After about fifteen minutes I realised she had drawn out of me a great deal of personal information but revealed nothing of herself. She was wearing dark glasses and so I could not see her eyes. Then her boyfriend arrived, a huge Mexican, he gave off bad vibes without even speaking. She left and he sat down next to me and immediately began to aggress me. He boasted to me how experienced he was with ayahuasca and how he was basically a shaman himself, running San Pedro and peyote ceremonies. Amongst other things, he said that westerners shouldn't be taking ayahuasca, they had no right. This attitude was certainly problematic considering he was at an ayahuasca retreat full of westerners! But it wasn't so much what he said but the palpable negative energy he exuded. His name was Eduardo; I later nicknamed him Eduardo el Diablo! When it came time to drink our tree bark tea he made a big show of praying over his. He seemed to position himself in the centre of the room, attempting to dominate everyone including the shaman. I tried to be non-judgemental but by this stage it was proving difficult. That night in the ceremony he was to show his true colours. It so happened that that night in the ceremony he was placed next to Michèle and from the very start he was arrogant and disrespectful. We had been asked never to point our feet towards the mesa out of respect, he immediately did just this and despite being asked several times, he refused to stop. It reminded me of a satanist going into a church and turning the crucifix upside down. After drinking the ayahuasca he became extremely restless constantly moving and agitated. In an ayahuasca ceremony your personal space is sacrosanct. No one touches you except the shaman or helper, as all the senses are altered by the plant. Soon he began to touch Michèle, rubbing his hands on her and talking. She had to repeatedly ask him to desist but he carried on. Eventually when Michèle was purging he demanded she give him her basin because he had lost his. In fact by insisting on having his feet pointing the wrong way he had actually kicked his bucket onto the mesa! Michèle of course said no, as she was purging but he snatched the bucket from her forcing her to vomit in her hands. This was such a disrespectful act particularly as you really don't want to touch what you are getting rid of with ayahuasca. Then he proceeded to turn around and vomit all over the person on his other side. It was like the devil had been given a cup of holy water to drink, it was like something from the Exorcist movie! The next day he was confronted but claimed that he had no recollection at all of the ceremony. Well, amnesia isn't normal with ayahuasca and nor was his reaction to it. That day, the woman came in and said they were leaving. This time I got to see her eyes and I didn't like what I saw. They hadn't come for purposes of healing or spiritual growth but rather to try and disrupt this from happening.

Another time in Peru, in Pisac, I was sitting at a table in my hotel courtyard, writing notes for this book. A woman came and sat at the table. She was wearing a long flowing white robe, malas and a turban. The type of clothes that say, *look at me, I'm really spiritual.* After a while I saw that 'subtle something' in her eyes, the same as with the woman at the ayahuasca retreat. It was as if she knew what I was writing about and had come to create doubts about everything I had experienced. She said that she was a kundalini yoga teacher so I shared that I'd had an awakening. She then said that she would never want one and that all true yoga teachers will tell you the same. I thought why call it kundalini yoga then, why not just call it exercise. She then said that people are always trying to climb ladders of experience. I write quite a bit about ladders in shamanism here. She then went on to criticise everything about ayahuasca, so that was a large part of my spiritual life thoroughly dumped upon! Actually, she really got under my skin as this was all delivered with a very calm sweet demeanour, which was utterly fake. It's what I call the 'namaste and fuck off' syndrome. In an ayahuasca ceremony a few days after meeting her I had a dream, this is the only time I have dreamed after ayahuasca. In the dream Michèle and Dougal came running to me saying that the woman had captured some beautiful birds. Parts of my soul that have separated often take the form of birds. We found her and it was clear she was going to kill the birds. We rescued them and Dougal chased her off. This dreamed confirmed for me what I had sensed looking into her eyes.

During dieta in the retreat a strange but also quite funny thing happened. I was relaxing in my hammock when suddenly a face appeared before me. It was red; with a pointed chin, a black goatee beard, little horns and a big grin. In short it was the classic face of the Devil. Immediately a point of energy came up from my root chakra, up my spine and shot out of my third eye into the centre of this devils grinning face. The face then exploded into myriad teardrops of liquid and was gone. I feel that the demonic is here to divert us and test us. The word comes from Greek and one meaning is inner self. To sin, means to miss the mark. We must have a sure and ruthless aim to annihilate and transmute our inner demons.

CHAPTER TWENTY-ONE

THE BIG BODHISATTVA

It is often said in spiritual circles that when you are ready the teacher will appear. Having had the experience with a false teacher I was reluctant to ever put myself in that position again. A yogi whose wisdom I respected had written a piece on the Internet where he said that the grace of the guru was essential for spiritual unfolding to occur. I wrote to him relating my own experience, my concerns and asked was the guru really necessary. His reply was most interesting and I think really amazing. He said that yes, the grace of the guru is absolutely necessary but that you must on no account seek the guru, it is the gurus job to find you. Furthermore, you may receive the grace of the guru and be completely unaware of it. Finally, he added that the guru, need not even be in human form. Well, my guru certainly did find me and he definitely wasn't in human form, he was a dog, called Dougal!

Our first dog Noisette had been dead a couple of months and I was beginning to miss having a dog. Noisette had been quite a difficult dog, she was a bearded collie and delighted in chasing sheep, rolling in anything that smelled disgusting and eating things she shouldn't. Once she ate a pincushion and we spent hours extracting pins from her gums. She also ate watches, shoes, furniture and walls, but she remained with us for thirteen years. Thirteen years of Noisette had turned us firmly into cat people but I knew another dog must come into our lives. We began to consider what kind of dog we would like and all I knew was, it couldn't be another bearded collie and it had to big! It was Michèle that remembered a dog we had seen at a hotel in Brittany many years before. It was a distant memory but we both remembered the dog as being remarkable and Michèle actually even recalled the name of the breed, a Leonberger.

A Leonberger it turned out is one of the largest dog breeds in the world. It was created in the town of Leonberg in Germany in the 18th century. The towns' coat of arms not surprisingly is a lion and they decided in honour of this to try and breed a dog that resembled this huge feline! A Leonberger is essentially a cross between three giant breeds of dog, the Newfoundland, the Great Pyrenees Mountain Dog and the Saint Bernard. Fully grown, they have a long coat of golden hair and a black face. They weigh up to eighty kilos and in my opinion look a bit like a bear, pretending to be a dog. If you want to get an idea of Dougal watch the film, 'Call of the Wild' about a dogs yearning to return to his wolf ancestors. A Leonberger is the star of this film. Despite their huge size and strength they are amongst the sweetest and gentlest of all dogs and it was this reputation that was a deciding factor for us. We began to look for one of these monsters and despite being quite rare we found a breeder in our locality. Puppies were due on the seventh of December, our daughter's birthday, it felt like a sign.

At this point I was just at the beginning of my spiritual journey in adult life, taking my first tentative steps back into yoga and meditation. After we found out that puppies were coming I had a dream. I was standing in a forest at the bottom of a high cliff. On the top of the cliff was a Leonberger. It jumped off the cliff and landed front of me. It said, *I am a shaman Leonberger*. I told Michèle and we laughed but in truth I thought little of it. I really had no proper idea what a shaman was at this time and it wasn't until after Dougal had died that I remembered this dream.

After Dougal was born he had to stay with his mother for two months but we gave him a teddy bear imbued with our scents so that he would be used to our smell when he came to his new home. I should have known he was into shamanism, as the poor teddy got thoroughly dismembered! When Dougal came to live with us at two months old, he became best friends with our little foundling Siamese cat Singha. They would tear crazily around the living room creating mayhem; we called them the 'fun loving criminals'. They remained firm friends even when Dougal had grown to vast proportions. Sometimes he would carry her gently in his mouth, we would see them going by, Singha hanging limply held by the skin at the back of her neck like a kitten in her mothers mouth.

Dougal grew up surrounded by felines, mad little bodhisattvas that would steal his food, use him as a bed, become accomplices in the stealing of cheese. They would bring their huge gentle god offerings of mice. He was too polite to refuse and would take them in his mouth, storing them in his cheeks to be disposed of later when no one was looking.

It was Dougal who brought me my first shamanic gift from the land, the pair of small antlers. I'm sure that he, as the actual shaman felt that they were really his. As I took them out of his mouth he gave a look as if to say, *OK, you can have them but remember it was me that went into the woods, rooted through all kinds of disgusting stuff, found them, and dragged them all the way here!* Weather permitting I would always meditate under the oak tree and Dougal would always come with me and sit silently until I was finished or come and give me a nudge if I was taking too long. One time I came out of a very deep meditation and nearly jumped out of my skin because the head of a baby deer had been placed at my feet. Dougal, sitting silently a few yards away gave me one of his shaman looks. The night before I came into full awareness of the Tiger, I had a dream. I saw Dougal walking towards me with a Tiger, they were rubbing noses, he was bringing the animal to me.

One day I went to pick up pizza in town and as usual Dougal came, as he loved a drive in the car. I noticed he seemed to have difficulty launching his huge body into the car but thought he was just being lethargic. We went and got the pizzas and Michèle and I sat down at the table to eat, with Dougal at our feet waiting for titbits. I was about half way through eating when I noticed that Dougal was resting quietly with his chin on his paws rather than hassling us excitedly for pizza crust, as was the norm. I said to Michèle I thought he may be sick and then she noticed he was drooling which is something he never did. I immediately suspected a twisted stomach, which is something that happens to big dogs and brings a very fast death. I had him at the vet within fifteen minutes where it was discovered he had an extremely high temperature, and a severe infection. It was touch and go for a while and he ended up on a drip for three days. After a phone-call from the vet telling me that Dougal's condition was very serious I lay down in bed and looked for guidance. Drifting off into sleep, I saw myself playing my first drum. In front of me was my new drum and as I was drumming the spirit ongon would repeatedly shoot off as if from a bow and arrow towards Dougal. That evening I went outside to reenact what I had been shown. I drummed my first drum, which was tight and sounding perfect. After, I picked up the new drum to play and it was totally slack, the slackest I've ever seen a drum, it was like trying to drum something liquid. This was strange as both drums had been in the same room, in exactly the same atmospheric conditions, the fact that one was completely taught and the other completely slack made no sense to me. I realised that my first drum was driving the second and that the second was slack because the spirit was away working on Dougal. Dougal came home on Samhain and seemed fine for a while but really the treatment was just masking the symptoms of something much more serious. Despite further visits to the vet, the tumour in his bladder that was killing him remained undiagnosed and he died at home with us a few days after his sixth birthday.

That night I dreamed of a child, tiny pieces of white paper, like confetti, were thrown over it. The pieces changed first into flowers and then into butterflies. Then spirit women came with flowers tattooed on their hands and wrists. They took my hands and showed me that I had the same. Then I saw my whole left arm was covered by a tattoo of Quetzalcoatl, the feathered serpent marrying earth and heaven.

The next day I chose a beautiful place to bury Dougal near the oak tree. I went away to get my shovel and when I got back Singha was there, she knew it was Dougal's place. After digging I sat under the oak to meditate. Straight away the Tiger came, and I could see Dougal sitting down. The Tiger nudged him picked him up like a kitten and off they went. After burying him we covered his grave with stones and I played a lament I had written for him on the harp, Cumha MacDougall, 'Lament for the Dark Stranger'. During the night I felt weight on the bed behind me and the duvet pulled tight around me, from something heavy pressing on it but there was nothing there. I dreamed I was in a large empty house and fell asleep on a couch. In this sleep within the dream I began to sing, Dougal is gone, Dougal is missing, over and over. Then, still within the dream I woke myself up singing and was embarrassed to find I was not alone. Sitting next to me was a woman, she said, *this has clearly affected you very deeply but it's best to let it go.*

Dougal had died on the 13th of December and on Christmas night he came to say goodbye. I was awoken by the spirit of Dougal clamping his jaws firmly around the upper portion of my right arm. It didn't hurt, it was just to get my attention. I then fell back asleep and dreamed I was at home in Kent. From the side of the house Dougal came running at full speed. He was beautiful, his coat shiny and lustrous and billowing with the speed of his motion. I realised that in this moment I was truly with him again. We greeted each other with great joy and played together again for one last time.

Some say that shamanically, a domestic animal spirit does not have the power of the wild ones but I would argue that they offer something very different. Incarnating as a domestic animal like a cat or dog entails a huge element of risk as they are putting themselves completely at our mercy. I read a book on dog training by a man that had grown up in the Soviet Union. Under the Soviet regime it was incredibly difficult to obtain a dog and if you did manage, it was a requirement that if needed, the dog should be able to serve the state. This meant that all dogs were highly trained and cherished. When he came to the West this man was utterly shocked at seeing the amount of animals discarded in animal shelters waiting to be put to sleep. Domestic animals are in between the worlds; they forsake the call of the wild to be given the chance to give us their hearts. Dougal's great teaching was that for six years, all day, every day, he gave unconditional love. How many of us can say the same.

CHAPTER TWENTY-TWO

THE PHOENIX AND THE RETURN TO ISIS

As the winter solstice approached I knew the time was coming to enter into communion with the only other entheogen that has directly called me, that has been spiritually insistent that we meet, the mushroom *amanita muscaria*. Of all the entheogens this is perhaps the most mysterious and the original shamanic path through the wood to find this mushroom has other paths leading off towards such unlikely places as the medieval Christian church and the oldest work in the Hindu tradition, the Rig Veda. Far more capable authors have done first rate academic research into the vastness of this mushrooms influence on culture and religion all over the world. It is one of those almost unbelievable secrets hidden in plain sight and anyone interested in the bigger picture should read John Allegro's, 'The Sacred Mushroom and the Cross' and Wasson's, 'Soma-Divine Mushroom of Immortality'. Here, I am concentrating on shamanism and kundalini and so I will just touch only briefly of some these *amanita muscaria* mysteries as they relate to these subjects and my own direct experience.

This is the classic red and white spotted toadstool, the image of which is deeply ingrained in the western subconscious. We see it in fairy stories as children, surrounded by gnomes, elves, and other magical creatures. It is associated with the wildwood, the dark forest, the world of faerie that entices us, yet of which we are also afraid. It's the dark side of the fairy story, the place that if we go there we may never come back from. Certainly one of the reasons it is so deeply embedded in our psyche is that it may be a relic of an ancient shamanic past; of practices perhaps brought to Europe by our Siberian ancestors and in Siberia to this day it is still used for ritual purposes. Further contributing to the importance of this mushroom in our subconscious is the connection with Christmas, as virtually all the associated popular symbolism of this festival connects directly to shamanic practices in Siberia and other northern shamanisms. First of all, Santa Claus is red and white just like the mushroom. In England he is known as Father Christmas and has origins going back to the Norse god Odin. Odin was a shaman god that hung upside down from the Tree of Life to acquire his powers. The Tree of Life in the Norse myths was a birch, this being one of the trees that the mushroom lives in symbiosis with. It also lives in symbiosis with various conifers and it is from here that we get the Christmas tree. Underneath the tree we put our presents, which at one level are really the mushroom. On top of the tree is often placed a star, which is really the Pole Star, also a vestige of Siberian practice. In Siberian ceremony the shaman would climb through a hole in the roof of the yurt and from here we get Santa coming down the chimney. Traditionally the mushrooms would be dried over the fire and from here we get our tradition of the Christmas stocking. The idea, that whether you have been a good, or a bad little boy or girl, will effect the presents in your stocking, relates to how you approach the mushroom and what kind of experience you might have. Writing a letter to Santa telling him what you want relates to the shamanic practice of having firm intention before embarking upon a journey with a plant teacher. Then there is the reindeer connection. These animals are of utmost importance for northern peoples like the Sami. It is said that the shamans would observe the reindeer eating the mushroom and afterwards collect the urine and drink it. All toxins would have been filtered through the reindeers system leaving the shamans free to work with the mushroom with no ill effects physically. Hence Santa flies through the air pulled by reindeer.

So even if we don't realise it, most western people are intimately familiar with *amanita muscaria*. One thing that everyone knows about it is that it is deadly poisonous. Only the thing is, it isn't. There have in fact been very few recorded deaths from this mushroom and most fatalities occur from ingestion of misidentified species. *Amanita muscaria* contains ibotenic acid, which the body must convert to muscimol which is the psychoactive component found in this mushroom. The main problem is that eating the mushrooms raw can make you feel quite sick and be very hard on the liver but that said you would have to ingest quite a lot of them before you would get seriously ill. This mushroom is not like the better known, psilocybin magic mushrooms. These can be taken in large quantities and are used very disrespectfully like a party drug by many people. *Amanita muscaria* is not like that. Like ayahuasca, with which there are many parallels, it will never be used recreationally, it is far too strong and unpredictable. Those who approach it with anything less than total respect, usually swear they will never go near it again in their lives.

Northern forests are predominantly green places; there are not many other colours that catch the eye. *Amanita muscaria* with its beautiful orange-red cap and white spots stands out like a flashing neon sign saying, *come on in, have a bite to eat, we provide all night entertainment*! It is quite clear that *amanita muscaria* wants to be eaten. If it didn't want to be eaten it would be green or brown and disappear into the forest background. So how did it come to pass that *amanita muscaria* came to be regarded as a deadly poisonous mushroom. Perhaps certainly prudence may have played a part due to the possibility of mistaken identity. Then again, country people would have been familiar with their local flora and fauna and there would certainly have been those quite expert in picking and identifying mushrooms. Perhaps the activities of the Inquisition and later the genocide of the European witches was a contributing factor. Certainly the threat of torture and a horrendous death would have deterred people from having anything to do with the older ways of spirituality. Perhaps also they made up stories so that their children stayed away from the mushrooms, to protect them not so much from the fungi but from the dangers of association with them. Certainly the 'War on Drugs' has been going on a lot longer than is commonly thought. There is an intriguing theory that whilst on the one hand the medieval church was burning anyone with even a hint of shamanism about them, they were at the same time knee deep in it themselves through their own use of *amanita muscaria*. The religious aspects of *amanita muscaria* are explored in depth in John Allegros, 'The Sacred Mushroom and the Cross'. Allegro was one of the world's leading philologists and the curator of the Dead Sea Scrolls and therefore a man whose opinions cannot be easily dismissed. It is certainly worth entertaining the intriguing possibility that within the higher echelons of the church there was a secret *amanita muscaria* cult where the mushroom replaced the host as the body of Christ. The host used in the

Catholic mass does resemble the cap of a mushroom and with its beautiful orange red cap the *amanita muscaria* can certainly be seen as a suitable metaphor for the sun. As a boy I remember in mass that the priest himself would have a much bigger host than those given out to the congregation. This was placed in an object called the monstrance. When this was held up, the rays of the sun could be seen emanating from the host. This theory I agree does sound far fetched but there are numerous pieces of evidence from all over medieval Europe showing *amanita muscaria* mushrooms encoded into divine iconography. We will return to this later as it is particularly revealing concerning the connection between *amanita muscaria* and kundalini.

My personal experience with *amanita muscaria* can be seen as three-fold. First, the mushroom making contact via dreams and then making itself physically available to me. Secondly, my ingestion of the mushroom and thirdly, interaction with the spirit of the mushroom, post-ingestion, in the following days.

Again I had a trinity of dreams but this time they were widely spaced. In my first dream I travelled back in time and met a Cistercian monk in a pure white habit. He gestured to a clump of *amanita muscaria*, they were glowing. We each picked one and walked and talked. I took out a camera to photograph the mushrooms but the monk said no, that no one must know I was from the future. The mushrooms then disguised themselves by shape shifting into butterflies. The monk then said to me, *your current pope in the future, will resign his membership of the human race*. Pope Benedict did in fact resign and I successfully predicted that the name of his successor would be Francis. I sensed a secrecy here, a member of a religious order revealing something to me, but which must be kept hidden. This dream came about two years before I actually took the mushroom.

In another dream I found myself in a quaint English village. I went for tea and cakes in a cottage. All the cakes were decorated with little *amanita muscaria.*

Finally I dreamed Michèle and I were walking down a garden path and in the middle of the path was a glowing clump of really huge *amanita muscaria.* They morphed and shape-shifted covering the whole garden in a carpet of red geometric patterns. A few days later Michèle went to Ireland where to her amazement under the birch tree outside our sons house were lots of *amanita muscaria.* In all our years in Ireland we had never seen them before, they are just incredibly rare. This was too much of a coincidence to ignore, so with prayer and intention Michèle harvested them, dried them in the oven, preserved them in honey and brought them home to me. By the time of the solstice they had been resting two months in the honey.

Closer to the solstice I had a very strange experience. I sensed the presence of *amanita muscaria.* I felt what I can only describe as 'amanita kundalini' moving deep inside me and strange kriyas manifested. Wiping my hand across my face down to my heart I saw a beautiful bird sitting on a branch, with three different colours of light on its chest. I experienced myself as energy within the bird, as the kundalini of the bird. In Siberian shamanic tradition the upper world soul is said to become a bird and rest in the branches of the World Tree, in-between incarnations. I sense that this bird and the pink spirit bird that came when I was making my drum may represent this aspect of myself.

Coming up to the solstice had been very sad as Dougal had left us, but I was gifted with some beautiful and meaningful dreams. Reminiscent of my first *amanita muscaria* dream, butterflies returned. I dreamed of two large blue butterflies flying high above me. It seemed I was in a way flying them like a falconer does with a bird. I gestured with my hand, one came down and landed on my heart. In a second dream I heard the song, 'Love is like a Butterfly' then a huge pale green butterfly landed on my head. Butterflies are of course all about transformation and seeing mushrooms become butterflies and butterflies become flowers further emphasised this message. With me I feel that the butterfly and the amanita are intimately connected and that like ayahuasca, amanita knew I was coming and this was the chosen expression for communication.

I have to say that I was very nervous about taking this entheogen. The individual mushrooms all vary in strength and each person reacts differently. It can be a fine line between a spiritually beneficial experience and waking up in hospital in a strait jacket, not knowing why or how you got there! The day before the solstice I journeyed, I asked should I take the *amanita muscaria.* Then that night I had a serious of intense dreams and visions all concerning the mushroom. First I saw it being picked, then cooked over a barbecue, I could hear my stepdaughter singing in the background. Then I found myself running down a country lane. I could see a flying saucer sitting in the woods surrounded by trees and flowers. A woman pointed at the flying saucer and told me, *THIS is the advanced meditation.* I remember seeing a woodcut of witches dancing in a circle next to a fairy knowle. The knowle had windows in it and bore a remarkable resemblance to a flying saucer. I suspect there may be a connection between UFO's and *amanita muscaria.* In my final dream I heard a voice say, *let's take amanita now!* My third eye then opened into visions of swirling orange light.

On the morning of the solstice I went out with my reindeer drum and some dried *amanita muscaria* and sat under the oak tree. The recommended dose for a mild experience is three milligrams of dried mushroom. Due to the variation in individual mushrooms, it is wise to build up slowly, until you find the dose that is best for you. Having found myself very sensitive to ayahuasca I erred on the side of caution, as in this case I would be my own shaman. Although Michèle was to keep a watchful eye, there was no one equivalent to an experienced curandero to monitor the situation so I was conscious of safety issues. It has been suggested that the berserkers ingested large quantities of *amanita muscaria* before entering into their legendary rages and I did not want Michèle to have to deal with that!

I opened sacred space, thanked the mushroom and prayed over it. Then I began slowly to eat it, it tasted delicious still coated in honey. I didn't eat it all at once; I took things slowly, drumming in between bites. The day was stunning, the sun was rising and the fields were covered in frost. I thought a lot about Dougal whose grave was close by, but on the whole I kept a positive state of mind and felt honoured to be where I was, doing what I was doing. A lot of people report feeling some nausea after ingesting this mushroom but I felt no ill effects at all. Problems may arise if not enough of the ibotenic acid has not been converted to muscimol during the drying process and this can be hard on the liver. As a precaution, at the same time as eating the mushroom I ate some raw garlic and took some milk thistle tablets. The garlic neutralises any excess ibotenic acid and the milk thistle eases any liver difficulties. After about an hour and a half I began to feel drowsy so I lay down to sleep. The sleep was strange; sometimes I wasn't sure if I was asleep or awake. I constantly had visions of the mushroom in my third eye, I saw the T-Rex standing behind a line of *amanita muscaria*, I saw orange light-energy spiralling down from the sky. I had dreams that were so vivid that I wasn't sure if the dream was reality or my sleeping state the dream. This wasn't like a lucid dream when within the dream you become aware you are dreaming and can control it. This was like a reverse of dimensions. After several hours in this state I felt fine, lucid and had no problems walking. This is where we get to the part about shamanic use of *amanita muscaria*, the drinking of urine. Just as the reindeer would act as a filter for the toxins in the mushroom, so could the shaman. Sometimes the shaman would eat the mushroom and then others would drink the shaman's urine. In fact *amanita muscaria* can be filtered through the urinary system up to five times. Now personally I would rather drink my own urine that that of a reindeer or somebody else's for that matter, and that is what I did. In fact this was no problem for me at all as I have been drinking my urine for years as part of my yogic practice. I shall return to this in more detail later in connection with *amanita muscaria* and the Rig Veda. Drinking urine infused with *amanita muscaria* greatly prolongs the ecstatic experience. I now entered a deeply meditative state, my kundalini was highly stimulated, I was in full energetic awareness of the three chakras in my head, ajna, sahasrara and bindu, I was filled with white light. After a time I again drank my urine and the meditative state continued. By early afternoon I was up and about but was not fully back in the world till the following day.

During the night the spirit of *amanita muscaria* came in a dream. In the dream I was looking out of my bedroom window when a large bird appeared. It was the orangey-red colour of the mushroom. It then transformed so that its feathers were white with black flecks. Then it walked over to my cement mixer, which is also orange and mixed its colours. One half of its body remaining orange-red, the other half pure white. It then changed back to its original colour and walked off. After some research I realised that the mushroom was showing me its life cycle. *Amanita muscaria* emerges from the ground with white flecks of soil on it. Then the cap becomes orange with white spots and the stalk remains white. Eventually the white spots may wash away leaving a pure orange cap as the mushroom melts away. By starting and finishing orange-red before disappearing it was showing me the cyclic nature of existence. The next morning I awoke fully refreshed and energised with great clarity of mind and so impressed with how communicative the spirit of *amanita muscaria* had been.

The most ancient of the Vedic texts of India is the Rig Veda; it was preserved in oral tradition long before being committed to writing. Within it are contained over one hundred hymns to a mysterious substance called Soma. Soma seems to be simultaneously a god, a plant and a substance. It is possible that all these aspects combined in the form of an intoxicating, hallucinogenic drink. A great deal has been written speculating that Soma was in fact *amanita muscaria.* The theory goes that Aryan peoples came down from Siberia into what is now Iran (where the Rig Veda was composed), bringing their traditional use of amanita muscaria with them. Being neither a scholar of Sanskrit nor early Asian culture I do not feel qualified to offer an academic opinion on this matter. However, there are, on a spiritual level, certain intriguing connections and confusions concerning yoga, soma, shamanism and *amanita muscaria* that I'd like to explore.

The word soma is not only to be found in the Rig Veda, it also occurs in yogic tradition. In a kundalini-awakened person, digestion plays an important role in the process and many mysterious alchemies occur in the stomach. Here, soma refers to a substance produced in the gastro-intestinal tract. This substance is drawn up the spine into the brain where further mysterious processes transform it into a substance called amrita. This flows down the back of the throat and is either caught by the tongue or goes back down into the body to be recycled as I described earlier. In yoga this is referred to as the nectar cycle. Soma is mentioned and praised in the Hatha Yoga Pradapika in connection with kechari mudra. In yoga, the terms soma and amrita are used interchangeably, amrita can also refer to soma. I have already related my experience in the ayahuasca ceremony where I tasted what is sometimes referred to as 'the divine nectar of immortality', and its full body bliss inducing effects. The flow of amrita has continued long after its initialisation in the ayahuasa ceremony. So here we have the reality of a bliss inducing substance called soma whose production in the body is induced through kundalini awakening but may also be brought on through shamanic entheogenic use, in this case ayahuasca. In the Rig Veda we also have a bliss inducing substance called soma, which may be a plant. Is it possible that the soma of the Rig Veda is both the amrita of yoga and a plant? In my case it was kundalini combined with ayahuasca that stimulated amrita/soma flow, what about kundalini combined with *amanita muscaria*? What if the name soma was the word used both for the substance produced in the body and the plant or plants used to induce it? The mysterious processes going on in the stomach can be felt clearly by the awakened person. In the Rig Veda there are references to 'churning' the vats of soma. Before the ayahuasca ceremony that induced my soma to flow, my stomach was very active. As I lay on my back on the bed, it felt like my stomach was being stirred by a huge invisible divine spoon. Could it be that 'churning the vats of soma' is actually referring to divine metabolic processes occurring in the stomach as a result of awakened kundalini combined with entheogenic use?

One of the main arguments supporting the idea that soma may have been *amanita muscaria* is that there are various references to urine drinking in the Rig Veda. As mentioned earlier this is well established shamanic practice but it is also an ancient yogic practice called amaroli. Just the mid-stream of first urine of the day is taken.

> *'Discard the beginning of the stream of water because it has too much bile. Discard the end of the stream because it is worthless. Wholly enjoy the cool, middle stream. This is Amaroli in the opinion of the Khandakapalikas.'36*

Apart from general health benefits it is considered particularly good for stimulating the production of amrita/soma. My own experience of drinking *amanita muscaria* infused urine was that of a deeply meditative state including stimulation of kundalini and the bindu chakra, which is the chakra particularly connected to soma/amrita production. In the Rig Veda the impression is given of vast amounts of soma being drunk and produced and I suspect that repeated doses of amanita infused urine would certainly be capable of stimulating amrita/soma flow to occur.

So, to clarify, we have the word soma in yoga and in the Rig Veda. In both cases it is a substance capable of inducing divine states of consciousness. In both cases the drinking of urine stimulates this state. In yoga soma is produced as the result of aesthetic practice, urine drinking and the awakening of kundalini. In the Rig Veda it may be this same substance. Or it may be a plant. I suspect it is both, a plant that induces the production of Soma. Whether this soma is *amanita muscaria* or not I do not feel qualified to say only that it is powerful enough to be a soma stimulator.

One of the problems concerning the identification of *amanita muscaria* as soma in the Rig Veda is that it is described as a 'creeping vine', which it absolutely clearly is not. But only in the botanical sense, spiritually it can be perceived quite differently. Both ayahuasca and amanita are kundalini plants. The energy of both these plants rises up the spine. I suspect the description of soma as a creeping vine refers to the plant kundalini creeping up the spine, which is of course the real Tree of Life. In this way both ayahuasca and *amanita muscaria* can be seen as the 'vine' in the Divine.

Of the numerous depictions of *amanita muscaria* and other mushrooms in medieval churches from all over Europe, I find the Garden of Eden scenes most fascinating. In St. Michael's Church, Hildesheim Germany there is a painting dated circa 1192 AD. Here we see Adam on the right and Eve on the left. They are both holding mushrooms. In between them is the Tree of Knowledge/Life with a serpent entwined around the trunk moving upwards. The whole scene is superimposed over the cap of an *amanita muscaria*. This is a perfect representation of the kundalini awakening process with Adam as divine masculine uniting with Eve, divine feminine. In between them, the tree as the spine, up which the kundalini serpent rises. Whereas in yogic practice it is through spiritual discipline that the kundalini is caused to rise it is clear from this painting, as Adam and Eve are both eating mushrooms that the *amanita muscaria* is the initiator of kundalini here.

At Plaincouralt Abbey in the Indre region of France there is another illustration in a private chapel of the Hospitaliers. Again we have Adam and Eve and the tree. Only this time the tree is an *amanita muscaria* tree, with a large mushroom cap at the top and four smaller mushroom branches protruding from the sides. Again the kundalini serpent is ascending the tree. There is a mushroom near its mouth, which it appears to be offering to Eve. Adam and Eve are covering themselves with large *amanita muscaria* caps. Again this is a representation of kundalini awakening. The serpent offering the mushroom to Eve represents the kundalini, the divine feminine being the initiator, Shakti seeks union first with Shiva, as does Eve with Adam via the fruit of the tree. The fact that this is to be found in a prominent position in a private chapel of one of Christendom's elite military religious orders certainly suggests that at least some factions of the church possessed knowledge that was not disseminated to the congregation at large.

In the apse of the church of San Sadurni, Osomort, Spain there is a twelfth century mural painting. It shows Eve uniting with Adam by giving him a mushroom. Between them is the tree with six *amanita muscaria* branches. The serpent is absent in this scene.

The Canterbury Psalter from 1147 A.D has a really wonderful depiction with multiple layers of meaning. In the centre is the tree with the kundalini serpent curled exactly three and a half times around the trunk. The tree again is an *amanita muscaria* tree. With her left arm, Eve is passing a mushroom to Adam. With her right hand she is either receiving a mushroom from the mouth of the serpent or feeding a mushroom to the serpent. Both interpretations actually work and perhaps it is intended to be ambiguous. She may be feeding the serpent the mushroom to cause it to rise or the mushroom may represent the knowledge given by the risen serpent. As in my own case, it may be the awakened kundalini guiding her to take the mushroom. There is not just one tree in this scene, but three. To the left of Eve and to the right of Adam are also trees. The symbolism of these trees works on multiple levels. Each tree has branches from which various mushrooms/plants grow. The tree by Eve has six branches, the one by Adam five. Perhaps the artist didn't have room for six, it seems strange as the other two trees have six. Five and six do add up to eleven though, so perhaps there is a message there. The top of the tree by Eve has a white mushroom on top, the tree by Adam, a black one. Thus we see Adam and Eve as opposite polarities. Looking at the three trees from a yogic perspective we can see the them as ida, the feminine moon nadi on the left hand side, the central tree as sushumna and the tree on the right as pingala, the masculine sun nadi. In yoga these are regarded respectively as sun and moon channels. These two nadis must come into balance for kundalini to rise up the sushumna. This interpretation is backed up by another depiction in the psalter showing Jesus. Below him is a green and white serpentine band, at each end of which are sun and moon symbols. Resting on the 'serpent' is soil from which several mushrooms/plants are growing. Eve giving Adam the mushroom symbolises this process of unification. The mushrooms/plants on the two trees may be seen as the chakras up to the third eye, ajna chakra. Both these nadis intersect the chakras up the spine in a double helix, yet neither reaches the crown chakra. Only the central tree, which also has six mushroom chakra points, has the seventh chakra, the crown chakra, the place of divine union. Here the crown chakra (sahasrara) is shown as a red *amanita muscaria* containing smaller *amanita muscaria.* It strongly resembles the sri-yantra of tantric yogic tradition, considered to be the most accurate spiritual representation of the true nature of a human being. The sri-yantra expands outward and inward simultaneously and infinitely, sometimes the bindu point is included as the union of Shakti and Shiva within every cell of the awakened individual. Here, the bindu becomes the *amanita muscaria.* Two equilateral triangles can be discerned within the design forming a six-pointed star of *amanita muscaria.* An ascending triangle, crossing a descending triangle, representing the unification of opposites. As well as representing ida and pingala the outer trees can also be viewed as the individual spines of Adam and Eve. All three trees can be viewed as spiritually awakened spines. Just as in yogic/tantric systems the various different chakras are attributed different shapes and animals, perhaps here we see an ethno-botanical mycological chakra classification system.

It is generally accepted that western awareness of kundalini is something quite recent brought into more public awareness by the spread of spiritual systems from India, particularly the various yogas. What is astonishing is that these depictions from twelfth century Europe display openly a complete understanding of the awakening of kundalini to rival anything depicted in India. In the Indian depictions we often see rather complex almost scientific representations of the chakras and the nadis with kundalini superimposed over the human being. The European illustrations place the human firmly in a natural setting using trees, mushrooms, plants and animals to symbolically convey the message. This in itself is very shamanic. What is particularly interesting is that this complete knowledge of the kundalini process is in every case also presented in partnership with the entheogen, *amanita muscaria*. We also see that in some cases the tree of life also becomes an '*amanita muscaria* tree'.

It is easy to see why *amanita muscaria* might become identified with kundalini and enlightenment. Like the kundalini at the base of the spine, the mushroom in its true form as the mycelia lies at the base of the tree. Like kundalini it is invisible. The mushroom itself is a temporary expression of the true organism; although they appear separate they are all part of the one thing. In a dream I saw *amanita muscaria* pushing up through dark soil, I heard my voice talking about 'the mushrooms' plural, but then another voice said, *there is only ONE mushroom.* This is the great and beautiful teaching revealed in the Sanskrit texts, shown to me first by a grasshopper and now a mushroom, that there is only the One. The mushroom after reaching 'enlightenment', inverting into a chalice/grail shaped cup, melts, like the Oneness returning to itself. Various authors have identified the mushroom and its associated trees as being the true origin of the Tree of Life mythos and also as the source of the Grail legends. Truly though the spine is the original Tree of Life /Knowledge and the 'fruit' is the kundalini waiting like the mushroom for the right conditions of fertility to rise to the light. The awakened kundalini state is the true grail as the individual is turned into a vessel that can receive the divine.

I suspect that as with ayahuasca, the doctrine of signatures may also apply to the association of *amanita muscaria* with kundalini. Clearly the designers of these illustrations knew the science of kundalini awakening and would have known that no entheogen is actually needed in this process. The parallels of the life process of the *amanita muscaria* to that of kundalini awakening are many. This must have led people to the conclusion that it may also be a catalyst or inducer of kundalini. In all the illustrations, even when there are other kinds of mushrooms and plants present it is always the *amanita muscaria* that takes pride of place on the tree/spine as the kundalini plant par excellence. Both Wasson and the great psychedelic plant advocate Terence McKenna reported disappointing results with their personal *amanita muscaria* experiences. Both were investigating it as a possible candidate for Soma and were searching for a great visionary hallucinogenic experience of the kind attributed to it in the Rig Veda. McKenna only tried it twice which I suspect was simply not enough. Ayahuasca is definitely capable of inducing the states recorded in the Rig Veda yet many people drink it multiple times with no visionary effect whatsoever. Wasson tried *amanita muscaria* many times in different ways but got little more than nausea and tiredness. Wasson however was not a yogi or shaman and I think this may play a part. My own *amanita muscaria* experience even with a minimal dose was intense, the effects of which in fact lasted for weeks after. Both McKenna and Wasson were comparing *amanita muscaria* unfavourably to psilocybin mushrooms, but the effects of *amanita muscaria* seem to be very different. I suspect that this is a mushroom that comes into its own when taken by someone with a spiritually awakened nervous system, that has engaged in the necessary spiritual disciplines of meditation, prayer, yoga and fasting. Then, like ayahuasca it will act as a spiritual accelerant. The visionary aspect of awakening has always been considered a distraction by adepts of yoga and I sense that the spiritual qualities of *amanita muscaria* reflect this, that it brings awareness of the divine less through a temporary visionary state but through the awakening of kundalini. It seems likely to me that a highly sophisticated knowledge of the use of *amanita muscaria* akin to that which continues today with ayahuasca existed in 13th century Europe. The appearance of other mushrooms and plants in some of the illustrations suggests that like with ayahuasca, *amanita muscaria* may have been combined with other plants in a shamanic yoga system enabling the awakening of kundalini.

Nearly two weeks after the solstice the *amanita muscaria* was still very present. During meditation or before falling asleep the mushrooms would appear in my third eye. That sense of 'dark fairy-tale' was there, many mushrooms glowing at me in a dark forest. After falling asleep to mushroom visions, two big dreams further confirmed to me the connection between *amanita muscaria* and kundalini. In one I found myself walking through a tunnel. I could see light ahead and three sets of steps going up in front of a wall. One set went straight ahead, the others right and left. As I ascended the middle steps I could see so over the wall a vast endless still ocean. I was told there were two currents, cool to the left and warm to the right, at the centre where I was, these two currents blended perfectly. The corridor was obviously my spine, the sushumna, the stairs to the right and left, ida and pingala. The two currents blending perfectly in the centre, ida and pingala coming into equilibrium for kundalini to flow up the centre. I also felt that with me there was another layer of symbolism, that of yoga and shamanism blending into the form of shamanic kundalini. In the second dream I was aware of two corridors. They were built beautifully in stone and furnished and decorated. In between these two corridors was a huge stretch of ground that was being completely dug up; it looked as if a highway was being constructed. I found myself on this highway in a car with a friend. The friend was a musician and part of the old me I have been trying to leave behind, I associate him with old egotistical behaviours of mine. My friend manoeuvred the car, to make way for a formidable machine. It was a tunnel-boring machine, cylindrical in shape with a huge round mouth full of impressive teeth. I said in the dream, *'I wouldn't like to get in the way of that thing!'* Again here we are looking at the ida and pingala nadis as the corridors with the road works as construction being done on the spiritual highway of the sushumna. The dream was saying get your self/ego out of the way and let the serious work continue. I suspect the building contractor behind this work to be *amanita muscaria*.

In January I again fell asleep to visions of multiple *amanita muscaria* and received yet another important dream. I found myself in a desert-like moonlit place. I came to a small lake, the water looked magical, there were different colours in it, and it was very inviting. I felt I wasn't myself but a god-figure in a myth. I had a feeling that for some reason I wasn't supposed to drink the water or rather 'something' didn't want me to drink it. But I did, I kneeled, cupped some in my hand and drank. It was beautifully refreshing and further ignoring the feeling that this was forbidden I waded in and submerged myself fully. After this I found myself with a girl friend, she was my champion and carried a sword. Two Knights Templar came and with swords and daggers tried to kill us. We fought back and my friend with her sword defeated them both. The Templars here represent for me secret knowledge, but secret knowledge kept for the elite few. In their red and white costumes they are at once the *amanita muscaria* and repression of the knowledge of it. My friend as the goddess defeats them.

On Christmas Eve night the *amanita muscaria* bird once again came into my dreams. Its feathers were shining and beautiful, it sprayed warm drops of urine on my face (another confirmation it was connected to the mushroom) and nuzzled me lovingly. A man in the dream held open a book with pictures and names of different birds as if bringing to my attention that the identity of this strange bird was somehow important. This niggled in my head for the next few days and the word 'phoenix' began to become insistent. It would seem that in another great cosmic joke I had been pissed on by a Phoenix!

I was stunned at how via the phoenix and the life cycle of the mushroom that *amanita muscaria* revealed such a great teaching to me. I suspect that just as ayahuasca sometimes comes as an anaconda, that *amanita muscaria* comes as the phoenix and that rather than man, inventing the myth of the phoenix, that the phoenix is an avatar of *amanita muscaria* and that it has presented itself as such over millennia to those willing to undergo death and rebirth in the forest. We find an origin of the phoenix myth in Egypt with the bennu bird, associated with resurrection and the goddess. Mirroring the cyclic natures of the mushroom and the phoenix I find myself returning to the first line of this narrative, *I used to think it all began the night I dreamed of the goddess Isis*. Several months after Dougal had died, another Leonberger puppy was to come into our lives, his mother's name was Isis.

CHAPTER TWENTY-THREE

BLACK BEAR DRUM

'No one can understand the sounds of a drum without understanding both drum and drummer.'
The Brihadaranyaka Upanishad

Magical drums do seem to want to enter the world through my hands and another drum, this time from the far north of Europe made itself known to me. In a dream I saw many Sami people lined up before me, just looking at me. They are the last indigenous people of Europe and they make some of the most beautiful drums in the world. The drums are oval in shape and always decorated with many symbols representing a map into the cosmological world of the shaman, the noaide. In another dream I met a Sami boy who wanted to make a drum. We walked up a very steep hill together until we came to a music shop. I brought him in and the people there were very happy to see him and they went away to make a drum together. In a journey I saw six noaide, they held their drums in front of them like shields, I could see the complex designs on all of them. I began to sense something 'Sami' was coming through and finally the drum revealed itself in a most beautiful dream. In the dream, I was walking with a friend in a picturesque village. Ahead of us was a lovely white cottage overlooking a clear blue sea. I knew that magical people had lived in the cottage in the past and that it was a special location, I said to my friend, *this is the perfect place for me.* We crossed a small bridge next to the cottage and began to look for any signs with information about its history. My friend called me over, he had found two glass cabinets. The one on the left contained a book with writing in gorgeous ancient magical calligraphy. The one on the right contained an image of a serpent dragon spiralling upwards. I said to my friend, *that's kundalini!* Then I found myself sitting down cross-legged with an oval Sami drum floating in the air in front of me. It just emanated magic. I was looking at the drum from the back; I could see beautiful silver grey fur with subtle hints of glowing turquoise. It was decorated with huge bear claws. Then within the dream I received a vision of brown bears and black bears that used to roam the artic regions in ancient times. Then the drum began to play and it was the sweetest sounding drum in the whole world. Three crows and an eagle flew above me. Two days later I dreamed of the drum in a cave, it shone like the moon. On the floor of the cave was an ancient Irish horn made of gold, it was beautifully decorated with Celtic designs. Below the drum I could see the skin of a black bear, once again the drum began to play. I felt very strongly that this was to be a black bear drum but I was confused because in the first vision I was shown black and brown bears. After some research however I discovered that the species called the Black Bear has a slightly misleading name, as they can be brown as well.

That the bears in my vision inhabited the artic is significant in that the word 'artic' derives from the Indo-European word for bear. I discovered that the bear played a significant role in the culture of the Sami and many other polar peoples. The Sami call the bear 'ìsaivoî', which means sacred, and half of the seventy or so surviving drums have bears painted on them.

A few days later in a vision I saw myself cutting a skin for the drum. Then the drum was struck three times and the bear arrived, it was big and very black, further confirming the species to me. That night I had an extraordinary experience. Lying in bed I felt a membrane pressing down on me. As I moved my face forward I could feel my face pressing into it, that it was malleable. Something told me I should push harder and I felt my face push through it, then my spirit arms were tearing at it and I literally ripped myself through into another dimension. It was like something out of the Matrix movie, if anyone had seen this from the other side they would have been seriously freaked out. In fact, I could hardly believe I was doing this myself! In the caves of Peche Merle near my home there are prehistoric shamanic rock paintings. Some of these are simply hands. The great scholar Graham Hancock posited that perhaps these hands actually represent something pressing into the cave from an outside dimension. Based on this experience I think he may be on to something with this idea. In this new dimension there appeared before me a ladder made of silver light, which I began to climb. I realised I was climbing the ladder of my DNA. The effort was strenuous, and my spirit body felt sore. Upon leaving the ladder I saw something small flying in the distance. I followed and saw many little lights flying. They flew like a swarm of insects, they noticed me and came all around me. Each one was made of light but within each, were different colours. One came very close to me and at this point I came back to normal consciousness. The next night as I lay in bed I could see a tube of blue light ascending from my third eye up into the universe, inside it I could see the kundalini cobra swimming. Then I felt the membrane pressing on me again. I pushed with my face and went through. Above me was a great bear, it roared, displaying its impressive teeth. Then its aspect became kind and I found myself floating under the bear in a sort of vortex, spirits of all kinds were flying past me. Both these experiences were exhilarating but exhausting and posed many questions. One thing that occurred to me was that if I was capable of pushing through into another dimension, then certainly things from the other side could push through into this one, which further confirmed my suspicions that ET's and UFO's travel in this way.

The day after this, in a dream, I found that the singer Robbie Williams was living with our family. Despite being rich and famous he preferred just hanging out with us. At the end of the dream he gave me a book. I felt the book he gave me was this one, that I was literally being 'given' the book which made perfect sense to me as it feels like this book has almost written itself with minimal effort on my part. Then he gave me a cart, the type pulled by horses. I picked it up and walked with it like a horse. Spiritually speaking, as the horse is a metaphor for the drum, I think the dream was telling me to be like a drum, to be a gathering place for spirits, a bridge between worlds, a vessel for healing. I really couldn't figure out though, the spiritual significance of Robbie Williams. I don't really listen to much pop music and certainly would not in any way be classed as a Robbie Williams fan. Then it hit me as I remembered his song, Angels. The lyrics are very beautiful, speaking of the comfort of knowing you are watched over by a great loving presence. I had been visited by an angel! Later I dreamed of walking in a garden with my mother. In the middle of the freshly cut lawn I found the wing of an angel.

The next evening I sat down to meditate but straight away the bear came loping along. Then I saw a reindeer and heard someone singing 'Rudolph the Red Nosed Reindeer'! This got my attention and then a figure standing next to the reindeer launched an arrow into the air. I followed it as it arced high into the sky and landed in front of a spirit shaman that was making a drum. The figure began to stich, showing me the style of stitching that must be used and that this drum must be stitched clockwise. After all this I had quite a detailed impression of how the drum should be and set about gathering the ingredients. The Sami are reindeer herders and their drums are made from this animal. I still had enough left from the hide I'd used to make the Siberian drum and this was nice because the drums would be connected through the same reindeer spirit. I acquired an oval drum hoop, as this is the shape of most Sami drums and also what I was shown in the dream. I also knew that the drum must be trimmed with reindeer fur and be decorated with claws from a black bear. I have to say this caused a bit of a dilemma for me. The type of black bear that would have roamed Europe in times past is what is now known as the Asiatic bear, known in Tibet as the moon bear. Not only are they an endangered species but they are also poached and suffer greatly due to the demands of Chinese medicine, so there was no way I was going to consider obtaining claws from one of these bears. I then considered the black bear from North America where they are not endangered and hunting is legal and controlled. But then I read of a man caught smuggling parts of the animal out of Canada for the

Chinese medicine trade and in the end I decided I preferred bear claws to stay on living bears if at all possible! I know it sounds contradictory to have no problem with a reindeer skin but scruples over bear claws but there is a difference. The reindeer came from the Sami as part of their yearly cull. Their survival is completely dependant upon the reindeer and every part of the animal is used. The same cannot be said of the black bear, no one is dependant on the meat and fur of this animal. I do appreciate that some indigenous and other communities live in close proximity to bears and that they may have to be killed if they are a danger but this is not the same as commercial slaughter. Finally, I opted for high quality replica black bear claws. They are resin, made from casts from real claws and hand painted. They are so realistic that they have even fooled customs officials. After ordering the replicas, I was shown in meditation the huge black paws of the bear with its impressive claws, so I think the bear spirit approved. Following this I dreamed of being in a Sami tent with a noaide. I could see a Sami symbol drawn three times round a circle, the circle began to spin, I heard drumming, then woke up. A few nights later I couldn't sleep, I could feel very strong spiritual energy in me. As soon as I eventually did fall asleep, I left my body; I flew around the room and over Michèle before re-entering. I could see and feel my spirit body during this experience, it was made of thick viscous silver light energy, much like that which I have felt come into me on previous occasions. A while later I dreamed of a black jaguar, an animal with very lunar associations and I realised a big event was soon due, a total eclipse of the sun on the spring equinox by the moon. It seemed no coincidence that the Asiatic black bear is called the moon bear and that the drum in the cave looked like the moon. Michèle said that it was almost as if the bear was emerging from hibernation.

In a journey to discover more about the drum I was shown that it needed a solar symbol painted on it and that its front was to be divided into the three worlds. The spirit shaman then picked up the drum and held it in front of me. I could see the Tiger inside the drum, which then expanded into the tunnel and the Tiger ran down it. After this I dreamed of opening our beehive and pouring out a large jar of honey with tiny pieces of beeswax floating in it. The next day in meditation I had once again amrita flowing and I equated this sweet nectar with the honey but I also realised the association between honey and bears and that this must also be incorporated into the drum. The next night I dreamed of a vast cave situated near the top of a mountain. Michèle and I were living in it. With us, also living in the cave, were two bears, one black, one brown. Then we left the cave and walked down to a shoreline where a vast ocean of clear water was gently lapping. I dipped my toe in and it felt wonderful. I wanted to go in but a great train passed between the water and me. It seemed to be of infinite length and all the carriages connected by a cord. I thought how vast this cord must be and realised I was looking at my spine. I felt that although I was dying to plunge into the water a sense of responsibility was holding me back. I was standing on a shore the place where the land meets the water, the meeting point of different worlds. Shamanism involves maintaining balance between the earthly and spiritual realms, as such, shamans are intermediaries, with feet firmly planted in both places. In the Upanishads the seers talk of transcending the Tree of Life but as Eliade points out, the wood of the drum connects the shaman to the Tree of Life and I of course was making a drum. There is a sense that their intimate connection to the tree means that shamans forgo the final enstasis of the yogi and hold back from diving fully into that great ocean of consciousness. As the equinox eclipse approached I continued to sense that the veil between dimensions was very thin. One night I went outside and the sky was stunning, the Tiger appeared above me, a huge feline of light running across Orion over the walnut tree. Above the Tiger a single pearl of blue light appeared. Another night in my dream I found myself singing in Irish. My aunt Mary Brighid, my first spiritual teacher, the woman named after two goddess's appeared before me, she was glowing as the spirit animals do in my dreams. She was smiling and said, *you know you are singing sean nós, don't you?* Sean nós means 'old style' in Irish, and spiritually speaking, shamanism is the oldest style of all. She then said, *it's time to go now*, and disappeared. Following this in a shamanic state of consciousness I found myself holding Dougal's lead and I sensed his presence. I felt that Dougal should be free, but a voice said, *no, he wants to be with you* and then Dougal was there slipping his head happily into his collar. I have to say that these interactions with my mother, my aunt and my dog mean that the dead really don't seem very 'dead' to me at all.

The day before the equinox the reindeer skin that I had ordered arrived. I placed the drum hoop and the bear claws onto its thick luxuriant fur and I could see the drum of my dream becoming close to a reality. I sat next to the skin and parts of the drum and journeyed to see if there was any more the spirits wanted to show me about how it should be made.

The Tiger took me to a forest in the far north, we moved at tremendous speed across a snow covered landscape dodging between pine trees. A huge forest god came out of the trees towering above me. On some of the Sami drums in the Upper World portion we see these god figures, even taller than the trees they hold in either hand. This god was very angry at the intrusion and this is not surprising. The forests of Samiland, Sapmi, are incredibly ancient, they have been untouched since the last ice age. In these forests, the Sami have for millennia lived as reindeer herders. In a most humane system, the reindeer graze wild in forests full of trees hanging with lichen. Now logging is beginning to impact the region threatening the Sami way of life and the ecosystem of this primeval landscape. If I was the god of this forest I would be angry too. The god did let me pass and we then came to some people travelling in the forest. One of them showed me a drum. They showed me the handle and they wrapped reindeer fur around it and so now I knew how to incorporate this aspect. Then I saw one eye set in a face of thick black fur watching me, the bear was still making its presence felt. That night I dreamed of a dark haired woman, she came and sat on my bed and kissed me on the mouth for a very long time. I thought of Judee Sill and the kiss being a symbol of the union of opposites within us. In another dream a woman came and sang to me, her beautiful voice was crystalline clear and she sang to me in a strange language. Then she picked up a very big and powerful shamanic drum covered in Sami symbols and I realised she was a noaide and she was singing me a joik, a traditional Sami spirit song. As she played the drum, wonderful harmonics were generated and oscillated towards me. I heard the secret song of the drum that can be heard in the 'silence' between the rhythmic beats.

The next morning Michèle and I sat under the oak tree with our drums. Michèle drummed and I meditated as the eclipse progressed. After drumming, Michèle stood up and turned to thank the oak tree. As she did, at that very moment, two herons flew above us. Herons are solitary animals and it is extremely rare to see two together. To see two herons on a vernal equinox during a solar eclipse at the start of a new moon was a very magical experience. I felt they were like Michèle and I, on our great spiritual journey together.

Shortly before I was to make the drum the giant sloth returned in a dream. I found myself in a pet shop looking at a giant sloth. As I watched it stood up and shape-shifted into an incredibly tall sloth-man. Next I saw the sloth-man no longer confined in the shop but outside and free. He was receiving some papers as if he was graduating in some way. Next to him sitting on a chair was a man. He was completely engulfed in orange spiritual fire. I was aware that in some way he was responsible for preventing the graduation of the sloth-man up to this point. He was aware of this and asked to see the papers. Reading the papers he completely accepted the purification of the fire. I was aware throughout this that the sloth-man was me and also, that the man in the fire was an aspect of myself, and also that I was the witnessing consciousness of all this. The man in the fire had up to this point been holding back a very ancient shamanic part of me but was now accepting of his obliteration. I sensed no heat from the fire, spiritual fire is of a different quality, there was no pain. In the Bhagavad Gita

Krishna says, the yogis' way must be the way of fire. Like the Cathars that walked willingly into the flames at Montségur, we must never fear the spiritual fire of kundalini that burns away all that holds us back, all that we are not.

The day before I was to make the drum a golden light appeared to me in meditation. From this light came a queue of figures that began to enter my heart. There were so many and when the last one entered the Tiger was there, it had been guiding them into me. I lay down and my chest was filled with delicious warmth and I understood that these were soul parts returning to me. With aspects of me having been burned away and with others having returned I now felt ready to make drum.

Having seen the drum in the cave with the bearskin, I decided to re-enact this by making the drum by a cave I knew in the forest. Sitting quietly in amongst the trees on the reindeer skin, I stitched the hide to the hoop which I had painted sky blue. The skin had been soaking in well water in which I had placed *amanita muscaria* soaked in honey. The mushroom had been making its presence felt, and I knew it wanted to be included as the Sami and the reindeer both have a relationship with it. The honey was for the bee element and the association with bears. When I'd completed the stitching I hung the black bear claws inside the drum with strips of rawhide. Then I cut a length of reindeer fur and wrapped it around the handle as I'd been shown and suddenly the drum of my dream vision was before me. It was exactly as I'd seen it; it just emanated sacredness and power. For the beater, the symbolic heart of the drum, I attached a small roe deer antler to a handle of white wood and I tied this to the drum, as is the Sami custom. The antler was one of the pair that Dougal had brought me, the other had mysteriously disappeared. This reminded me of the dream vision I'd had before going to ayahuasca and it seemed right to name the beater, the One Antlered Stag. So the Black Bear Drum met the One Antlered Stag and the three of us sat together outside the cave in the forest.

Not long after I finished this drum, our new puppy came into our lives, another Leonberger, Duncan, born of Isis. We fell instantly in love with him and him with us. For the first few days he behaved like a perfectly normal puppy, playing, romping around and generally getting into all sorts of trouble. Then, he began to vomit and have diarrhoea, started to sleep a lot and stopped eating completely. He didn't respond to any treatment and ate nothing for five days. We were beside ourselves with worry and couldn't believe we might lose another dog. Eventually the vet discovered he had parvovirus. This should not have been possible as he had been vaccinated against it but it turned out that the breeder had been incompetent and had got the vaccination done too late. In fact he already had the virus when he was vaccinated and we had been given a seriously ill puppy. Parvovirus is potentially deadly and two of Duncan's sisters died. Usually death occurs in the first two days and if the puppy makes it through this there is a chance. By the time we discovered Duncan had parvovirus he had in fact already got through this critical period and after one night at the vet for treatment he was home and back to his normal rascally self. He was a very big puppy, even for a Leonberger, eleven kilos at two months, and although he lost a lot of weight during the sickness, it is testament to what a strong dog he is that he pulled through.

This was a very stressful time and the spirits were very compassionate to me, they knew I too needed healing. In a dream I found myself in bed, in the beautiful gardens of a spiritual retreat. A woman came to me, she was European, in her fifties with short grey hair. This unremarkable appearance concealed a truly magical healer. She placed a single finger on one of my vertebrae and this brought me into shamanic consciousness. Then she sent healing energy up my spine, which spread throughout my entire body in waves of love. Another day, I heard a voice say, *what do you want?*' I replied, *the best for all beings seen and unseen in all worlds known and unknown.* A noaide then appeared, he was made of golden light, on his drum was a zigzag snake and he carried a bow and arrow. He brought me to a shaman I know, Dawn Dancing Otter, she was seven feet tall. She touched my cheek, and said, *you have cried so many tears.* I touched my face and found it was streaked wet and that I had indeed been crying but had not realised it. She then enveloped me in a hug of pure love that felt wonderful. She placed her forehead on mine, and a spider web vortex of light opened, spinning sun-wise, as our third eyes merged into each other. When it finished I felt amazing and she just stood there looking down at me smiling. After this I began to dream of bears. First, the black bear of the drum came to me, he opened his arms and we hugged. Then I dreamed I saw him walking into a vortex of light, he disappeared through it as it exploded into all the colours of the rainbow. After this I saw the polar bear, reared up on two legs, a rainbow passing through him. I discovered that the skin of a polar bear is actually black and that this 'white' bear, is in fact also a black bear.

I was very grateful for these comforting and supportive spirit communications and I was sure that the spirits had played a role in Duncan's recovery, as he had not really received any proper medical treatment. In fact, I had taken a great journey to seek healing for him. I went down the tunnel and a monumental stone entrance was before me. Through this I could see the snow capped mountains of the Lower World. Waiting for me was a group of tigers. I went through and they surrounded me, like bodyguards. Nothing dared come near us as we travelled through the snow to a forest. There, we met Sami noaide, who performed healing ceremonies for Duncan. After Duncan recovered I did a ceremony giving thanks to the spirits, it was then that the Wild People came but I will talk about this in the following chapter.

One night I dreamed Michèle had taken me to a shamanism workshop. I had my black bear drum with me as we entered a large house. I put the drum on the floor, sat on it and zoomed off at high speed. We entered a room where a European shaman was waiting. He took my drum, made some adjustments to it, then said, *let's do some cleaning*. He then burned exquisite smelling herbs in a metal container and walked around the room smudging and throat singing at the same time. Then I saw another shaman, he was Mongolian and dressed in blue silk. He was performing ritual actions as the other shaman moved through the room. Looking around I saw that the walls were covered in shelves, which were full of hundreds of toy animals and dolls, like ongons. I then realized that they were alive, they were moving and handing candles and other ceremonial items to the shaman. Suddenly, I came into shamanic consciousness and I understood that these were all my shamanic helper spirits. They surrounded me, vibrating and chittering with excitement.

It seems strange that these drums should choose me to bring them into the world. I'm very conscious of cultural misappropriation and am very aware that an Irishman making a Sami drum might be viewed in this context. All I can think of is that in the same way that ayahuasca has now irreversibly pushed beyond her cultural and geographic boundaries, the same can be said of the drums. The first sense that awakens in the womb is sound, the first sound the fetus hears is the drumming of the mothers heartbeat. Sacred drums literally re-connect us to the Mother. The spiritual potential for positive change contained within these drums is just as real as that in ayahuasca and as such the universe is bringing them out into the wider world. The word mantra means ‘mind tool’ and the mantras of the Vedas are said to have been divinely revealed. I sense the same with shamanic drums, that they are revealed by Spirit, as tools to be made, for the spiritual enrichment of the world.

CHAPTER TWENTY-FOUR

THE WILD PEOPLE

Amongst my many spiritual encounters, those with the Wild People hold a special place in my heart. Bigfoot and the Yeti are perhaps the best known of these but there are many others. Some of those searching for them are looking for a great ape but this is a mistake, they are people. This is why I don't consider them as power animals. The traditional words for them make this very clear. Yeti means 'mountain man' in Nepalese. Almas means 'wild-man' in Mongolian and Sasquatch comes from the Salish sésquac, again meaning 'wild-man'. It is clear that the various peoples that came in contact with them did not regard them as animals in the traditional sense. It was in 1953 that Sir Edmund Hillary brought the Yeti to the attention of the wider world, after he came across large footprints in the snow, at high altitudes in the Himalayas. Likewise, it was through the Patterson-Gimlin film, in 1967, that Bigfoot entered into popular culture. Yet reports of these cryptid hominids are by no means a new phenomena. There are many tales of wild people from all over the world, including Europe, going back hundreds of years. In the Pyrénées mountains close to my home, there are many such stories. This region has many well-documented cases not only of Wild People but also feral children. The inhabitants of the area have historically lived in close proximity to bears up until recent times and knew well the difference between a bear, a feral child and a Wild Person. As recently as 1993 we have the following account.

'A group of speleologists prepared to spend the night at the ruins of a church near Collada de Vallgrasa in the Catalan Pyrenees Mountain Range of Spain. They heard strange noises resembling those of an enraged cat. When they came close to the church's large doorway, the scientists saw a frightened, weird, shaggy creature, approximately 1.5 meters flee from the building. He was of enormous bulk. The wild man appeared again in the woods between Farga de Bebié and Ripoll (Gerona). Two hairy beings pounced on two paleontologists then ran away from them.'37

In France we see again, that the traditional words for these beings indicate that they are people. In the Haute Ariège the Occitan word for the wild man is omé pelut, which means 'hairy man'. It is surely no coincidence that the Yokuts of California called the being today popularly known as Bigfoot, 'Hairy Man'. On the Tule River Indian reservation in the Sierra Nevada foothills there is a site called Painted Rock. In a rock shelter amongst pictographs of various animals is a depiction of a Hairy Man family. The Hairy Man himself is eight and a half feet tall, the mother six feet tall and the child four feet tall. These pictographs are approximately one thousand years old. The Tule River Indians have confirmed that Hairy Man and Bigfoot are one and the same being.

I'm not going to discuss here the evidence for the physical existence of these beings, as there is a vast amount of research available on this subject and my interest is primarily in their spiritual aspect. I am however, personally convinced, that they are here with us in ordinary-reality. They do most certainly exist in non-ordinary reality and my own experiences with them lead me to believe that they have a special relationship with shamans.

To this day Hairy Man remains of great cultural importance to the Tule River Indians as protector, healer and guide to the next world. It is therefore not surprising that tribal elders have been reluctant to talk too much about this. However, we do know that among the Yokut, Hairy Man was indeed connected to the shamans, but that a Hairy Man shaman was extremely rare and unusual. The subject of a Hairy Man shaman was in itself very sensitive and so little is known about what specific powers such a shaman might have had. The elders told just one story, in which Hairy Man comes to give his healing power to the shaman. In the story Hairy Man insists that the power he will convey must only be used to cure and never to cause harm. It was also said that the shaman would make an amulet in Hairy Man's likeness, swallow it and use Hairy Man as a bringer of dreams. It was in the world of dreams, journeys and visions that the Wild People initiated contact with me.

Of these Wild People it is the Sasquatch and the Almas that have honoured me with their presence. I sense that Sasquatch is connected to the Native-American medicine man aspect of my udha. I first encountered Sasquatch in a shamanic journey. He was eight or nine feet tall, he bent down on one knee to look at me. Later, in a vision, as I stood facing the woods, a large creature walked upright through the trees in front of me. There was not much space between the trees, it was like watching a shadow repeatedly emerging then disappearing. I could see thick dark hair and sensed great power. It then stepped out into a clearing, it was Sasquatch and he turned to face me. Although he exuded tremendous physical strength, he showed no aggression and I felt no fear. It felt like he was simply presenting his existence to me. Then, I was given some special green herbs and plants and told that they were for contacting or shapeshifting into Sasquatch. I went deep into some forest caves and found him sleeping. I stroked his face with the plants and he opened his mouth revealing formidable white teeth. Somehow, I knew I must put my hand into his mouth, to show trust. I did and he opened his eyes and gave me a vision, showing that we have a deep connection, that part of me is in fact Sasquatch. I found myself in a primeval forest of very tall straight trees. Through the trees I could see a large rounded green mound, covered in moss and grass. I could see that my arms and hands were covered in thick hair. There was no sound or thought, just utter stillness of mind and environment, I was aware that this was home and I was my ancient Sasquatch self.

The Almas are the Wild People of Central Asia and Southern Mongolia. Many stories come from the Altai Mountains, again re-enforcing the link with shamans, as the Siberians say it was there, that all shamanism originated. Local children are said to often see Almas children and that there is no fear between them. The Almas are certainly connected to the Siberian shaman aspect of my udha. They came to me after a time of great stress when my two-month old puppy, Duncan, nearly died. The spirits certainly played a big role in his healing and when he was better, I went out and did a ceremony, singing out my heartfelt thanks. That night the spirits responded with a spectacular display. It began as a dream where I found myself standing in the kitchen of our house with Michèle. Suddenly I became aware of a figure standing against the glass double doors that lead onto the patio. I felt a sense of recognition, and shouted to Michèle, *'look, they're back!'* This brought me into a shamanic state of consciousness, a state of total awareness in which I was fully immersed within the vision and I was filled with wonder and excitement. The being at the window was about five feet tall and of a squat muscular build with no neck. It had its back turned to us revealing a body covered entirely in short grey-blue hair. Although I was behind it, I could simultaneously see its face, which was hairless with a sloping brow. It was like a small wild-man, a miniature Sasquatch and I 'knew' absolutely this was one of the Almas. Then I saw three other figures, also about five feet tall but these were wearing shaman costumes. No part of their bodies was visible, the costumes covered their faces down to their feet. The costumes had ribbons in the colours of the rainbow on them, like those used by Siberian shamans. They each held drums, and as they drummed they spun around, the ribbons swirling around them. Three Siberian, Almas shamans, drumming and whirling like dervishes on my terrace!

The height and build of these shaman Almas corresponds to the traditional descriptions of them being between five and six and a half feet tall, not gargantuan like Sasquatch. It has been suggested by the great cryptozoologist Dr. Bernard Heuvelmans, that the Almas may be a surviving population of *homo erectus*. Not only do the caves of my region contain some of the worlds oldest shamanic art but they have also yielded a treasure trove of hominid fossils. Of particular note was the discovery of Tautavel Man a species of *homo erectus* living four hundred and fifty thousand years ago, the ancestor of the Neanderthals. Some reconstructions of Tautavel Man do match very closely the appearance of my Almas. I think the Almas came to me, as they have such a close connection to the region where I live, they too are of this place and are still here, at least in spirit form.

Being somewhere between the animals and us, the Wild Peoples are in a sense, like shamans, between worlds. For me they are my shaman ancestors. The message I receive from them is, *we are a part of you, that you have forgotten, and need to remember*.

CHAPTER TWENTY-FIVE

LIVING IN THE SACRED ILLUSION

I feel clear water splashing on me, and wake up. I realise its ice-cold Shakti pouring from my third eye onto my face. I see the Tiger and small birds fly up into the air. A voice says, 'Only one who can define themselves, then let go, can fly with the shaman'.

We live in an illusion but it is sacred and what we do here matters. Through my music I was very fortunate to connect with Josephine Fire Lame Deer. Like me, Josephine is a little between-worlds, in that she was raised Lakota Sioux but with a Scottish mother. I was honoured that she gifted a copy of my clairseach CD (Cumha), to her mother as a birthday present. Josephine has inherited a formidable spiritual lineage, being the daughter of Archie Fire Lame Deer and the granddaughter of John Fire Lame Deer. It is clear to me that the wisdom of these great medicine men continues to flow strongly out into the world through this medicine woman. I love the way Josephine expresses the ideal way in which we should live. She says,

'It is not what ceremonies you have, but that you pray...it is not what species you are but that you respect ALL your relations, rooted and skinned alike...it is not who your ancestors were but how you conduct yourself in this lifetime.'

In a dream/vision, I found myself at the source of a river and ahead of me I could see the kundalini serpent swimming through it. I observed that in the distance, the river turned in its course and flowed back towards me. I understood that I was responsible for maintaining the purity of this source, that what I allowed to flow from me, into this river of consciousness, not only flowed out into the world but also returned to me. This is why it is so important to always strive towards higher consciousness, even though this may seem very difficult at times. How we conduct ourselves in this lifetime, is of course affected by the main aspect of the illusion, that of separation. This is reinforced by the values of western society and in turn leads to cumha. As a professional musician on the road I have on occasion been witness to the sadness of cumha in others. I remember once playing in a small French village. There was a little fair on the village green and a marquee had been erected for the concert. There was a very strange and sad atmosphere in this place. Sitting alone on a bench on the edge of the green, away from where everything was happening was a hugely obese woman. She sat like this for several hours before the concert, talking to no one and no one talking to her. When we started playing everyone sat on chairs around the edge of the dance floor, no one came close to the stage, no one danced, no one talked or smiled. I sensed that they yearned to do all these things but something just held them back. One woman in her mid-thirties danced all night, but she would not come into the marquee, she danced alone in the entrance, between worlds. Then I noticed the obese woman, sitting at the side. She couldn't dance, I think she could barely walk but her head moved from side to side with the music and she was smiling, cumha-less, for a moment. An old man sat immobile all night until near the end we played Country Roads by John Denver. Then he was up like a shot, dancing passionately with a vigour that belied his years. After Country Roads he sat down again but at least for a few minutes he too had broken through his cumha.

Shakti through her power of Maya tricks us into forgetting we are One. Yogic tradition teaches that the human being is like a series of sheaths or like the Russian dolls that fit into each other. At the centre of our being is a tiny fragment of Spirit and surrounding this is the soul. Surrounding the soul is the mind and surrounding the mind is the body. The body is essentially a means for gathering information. My friend the Sanskrit scholar Susan Ferguson describes the body as a data-collecting vehicle. It relays data back to the soul for Spirit to experience. This is done via the five senses, which are the tools of Maya, the five serpents that bind us in their coils. If the line of communication were just body, direct to soul, there would be no confusion as to our true nature. The 'problem' lies in the fact that between the body and the soul is the mind. The mind is really a tool for interpreting the data brought in via the five senses but what happens is that the experiences brought in are so sensual, so overwhelming that the soul begins to identify outward towards the mind instead of inwards towards Spirit. Eventually the soul thinks it IS the mind. A good analogy is that of NASA sending out a probe to the Moon, Mars or deep space. The probe (body) collects data (five sense experience), which is interpreted and converted into images by a computer (the mind) and displayed on a screen. Imagine then that the person in NASA begins to identify so much with what they see on the screen that they forget who they are. We might consider them at best deluded, at worst mad but this is exactly what happens to us! This is why meditation is essential for those that want to take the journey home because meditation weakens the soul-mind connection and strengthens the soul-Spirit connection.

There are those who say the illusion is *only* an experience but the spiritual messages given to me do not support this. So many times in dreams I find myself in classrooms or colleges and other educational establishments. I sense we are in school and will remain so until our desire to graduate aligns us with the frequency of Love. It might be unnerving to some, but I also sense strongly that we are closely observed. In altered states of consciousness I have been purposely shown spiritual machines like cameras or drones following me around as if to say, *we are watching, don't say you didn't know*. In a dream I turned my Sami drum around to find the front had become a peacock with its tail fully opened, there are a lot of eyes in a peacock's tail! In a winter solstice vision I looked out of a window in my house to see the Tiger walking in the field. As I walked through the house, the Tiger was at every window looking in at me, nothing was hidden from the eyes of this Tiger. Ultimately of course, this is the One soul, in a myriad of forms, observing itself in myriad forms. Not only is nothing hidden but also everything we do is recorded. Once I journeyed to the place known as the Akashic Records, it was a limitless library with endless bookshelves. Quite quickly I found my own book, on the spine I saw my name, followed by a long series of numbers, all this was written in golden light. What was really interesting was that the numbers were constantly changing at tremendous speed; it wasn't a countdown, they were ascending and descending. I understood that the story of my book was being recalculated and re-written with my every thought, word and action and that I was entirely responsible for the potential outcome.

There are two interlinking paths of consciousness described in this narrative, the path of kundalini awakening via the self-initiation of yoga and the shamanic path of consciousness via initiation by spirits. I related earlier my vision of the Vertical Pillar of Light, intersected by the Rainbow Bridge. The Vertical Pillar of Light as the kundalini awakened spine is the natural yogic impulse within the individual to reach towards higher consciousness and oneness. The Rainbow Bridge I see as the shamanic aspect, the DNA, stretching out into the world, bringing higher consciousness down here and integrating it into the experience, *Earthing* it. Our spiritual experiences of higher consciousness and oneness are essentially meaningless if not integrated here. There are spiritual teachers out there, great 'masters' making a lot of money telling people, do not worry, everything is as it should be. They will tell you it's all illusion, of no importance, that there is no work to do, you already are what you seek. Well this kind of enlightenment is of no use to the world; higher consciousness must transform us into beings that actually care in a practical way. There is as much wisdom in Black Elk Speaks as there is in the Bhagavad Gita. The great Eastern teachings are like the Vertical Pillar of Light in my vision, a highway to higher consciousness but there is a danger of leaving Mother Earth behind. Indigenous wisdom traditions are like the Rainbow Bridge, spanning the Vertical Pillar of Light bringing higher consciousness back down into unification with nature. The shamanic path of consciousness reveals the Spirit that moves through all things. The yogic path of consciousness reveals that you ARE the Spirit that moves through all things. Although the various spiritual paths may sometimes seem to contradict each other, the various truths they profess often make sense when superimposed upon one another like the three shamanic worlds. Mongolian shamanic souls oscillating through holes in a central axis, Indian nadis criss-crossing sushumna, double helix DNA serpents, snake-like vines climbing tree/spines. There are many tributaries of truth running into the World River and we are tributaries to the river ourselves which runs both from and to us. The shamanic teachings of the directions and the gol reveal that we are always at the centre of all this. Black Elk said,

> *'The first peace, which is the most important, is that which comes within the souls of people when they realize their relationship, their oneness, with the universe and all its powers, and when they realize that at the centre of the universe dwells Wakan-Tanka , and that this centre is really everywhere, it is within each of us.' 38*

Another aspect of the illusion is that the majority of us only ever consciously experience one reality, we live with a conviction that the material world of everyday existence is all there is. Michael Harner, an anthropologist and the founder of Core Shamanism coined the term Ordinary Reality to describe this state. The additional states of consciousness experienced by shamans, he calls, Non-Ordinary Reality. There are multiple layers of Non-Ordinary Realities as was revealed to me in a complex dream sequence. I found myself in a room in which there was a small box. A room is, in a sense, also a box, so, a box within a box. I was told to look through a hole in the box. Looking inside, I saw a strange but beautiful being, humanoid but not human. I watched as this being moved with incredible poise and grace in a whole different universe, contained within the box. Then I left the room and I was looking at a round table in the middle of an ocean. Sitting at the table was another strange humanoid, it looked both futuristic but also like a wild-man, it had something of the Almas about it. It said, *here, we answer the big questions.* It then reached into the ocean and pulled out a human skull. As it did this, I was aware of being both above and below the water simultaneously, I saw the hand entering the ocean from the top but was also the witness to it plunging through the surface from below. Once again the scene changed and I was looking at the entrance to a tunnel cut through the rock on the side of a mountain. In the tunnel were two strange beings of yet another kind. They were humanoid in shape but what was un-nerving about them was that they were made of darkness. They seemed one-dimensional, like silhouettes, it looked as if their shapes had been cut out of the canvas of ordinary reality with a craft knife, revealing a blackness so deep, it could swallow you. Then, moving with lightening speed, the two beings passed through the wall of the tunnel and disappeared. Although I was scared, I felt I was supposed to go after them and I found a door in the rock and entered into a small room. Here, there were cupboards, wardrobes and chests of drawers. I began to open doors and rummage through the contents, expecting any moment that one of the shadow beings would leap out at me, but this did not happen. Instead, I heard a soft female voice say, *did you really think we would ever let any harm come to you?* At this moment I shifted from being in the room to looking through a round portal, watching myself, still in the room. From this I understood that my consciousness exists at various different levels, that simultaneously I am both observer and observed and that I am loved.

The majority of the experiences I share here have been joyful but that is not to say that everything has been easy. Some of the kundalini phenomena have been rather scary both psychologically and physically and I thought I was dying in two of my ayahuasca ceremonies. The dredging up of the really deep dark stuff within us can also bring disturbing manifestations. For a time maggots kept appearing in my dreams, everything would seem normal until I would notice hundreds of them crawling on the floor and furniture. In one dream a couple came to see my house. In dreams the house often represents you, and the state of your subconscious. They said they were from the parsonage, which is a house for the clergy and therefore symbolizing a holy place. They looked around and said my house was very nice but there was a problem and they looked to a corner of the room. I followed their gaze and saw a bowl on the floor, it was red with white spots, like an *amanita muscaria* mushroom. I looked in the bowl and saw it contained some maggots, so I took it outside and emptied the maggots into the earth. Maggots are of course the start of the life cycle of the housefly which brought me the disturbing realization that this was only the beginning of something. Sure enough about a month later the houseflies came in dreams and I realized this was about a repetitive, cyclic behaviour that I had to stop repeating. It certainly didn't feel nice to know that I had something inside me that maggots and flies could feed from, in my otherwise clean house.

Other times, the knowledge that comes to me may simply make me sad. I might for instance be shown the outcome of a situation involving a person but know there is nothing I can do to change it, that it must run its course. One incident that upset me was discovering how distraught our dog Duncan was the first time we had to leave him. He was at home with his cat-friends and a person he knew was staying in the house to look after him, but he was still deeply affected. While I was away he came to me in a vision, he was so happy to see me but on his spine, at the location of the heart chakra was a deep wound. It was red and open as if someone had hacked at his heart with an axe. After this I would always tell him when I was going somewhere and when I was coming back. There was another upsetting time, when a fox systematically took one of our ducks every day. I don't resent the fox having the odd duck or chicken but not all of them! I was away from home and during the night I found myself in an altered state of consciousness back in my garden. The spirits of the ducks were running in confusion and panic. The fox was there with a duck in his mouth, I fought with the fox and freed the duck but it was too late. The fox then began to bite my hand repeatedly as the spirit animals so often do and then all of a sudden he let me put a leash on him and we were friends. I was very happy to have the fox as a spirit ally but the memory of the distress of my poor ducks has remained with me. The next day Michèle rang me up to say the last two ducks were gone, but of course I knew this already, because I was there. Then, there can be a certain feeling of loneliness also, as the kundalini process is so intensely personal and internalized, you cannot prove what you are going through and over time you learn that talking about it is not always for the best.

Indigenous peoples are rightly protective of their own words and spiritual traditions and are sometimes critical of westerners calling themselves shamans. Yet it is also true that the phenomena of kundalini awakening and shamanic awakening are universal, we are all human beings with equal spiritual potential. The difference is that indigenous people have retained knowledge and respect for these processes whereas in the west knowledge has been suppressed, lost and ridiculed. A person in a tribal situation experiencing the phenomena described here would likely be sent to the shaman and would most probably be recognised as one with shamanic potential and enter into training. In India, a kundalini awakening would be acknowledged as a great blessing. Once I saw an Indian man performing pranayama in a park. We got talking and when I mentioned my kundalini awakening, he bent down and kissed my hands. I felt like crying, as the response of this beautiful yogi was so different to that of anyone else I had shared with.

The west has no such structure to support the person in these processes. Talking to a doctor will result in heavy medication at best, incarceration at worst. The other choice is to find a spiritual teacher. This is in itself a minefield peppered with well meaning people who are misguided and not ready to be teachers to full-on predatory conmen out for sex, power and money. The main difference therefore lies in the support system and structure provided by millennia of tradition for the potential indigenous shaman as opposed to a society that regards the process as simply impossible and an indicator of madness. It is the initiations by Spirit that make a shaman not initiations by humans. The human initiations act as a support to the spiritual ones within specific cultural parameters. In my own experience I have found that in the absence of human initiations the spirits will perform something very similar in Non-Ordinary Reality. For example, there is an initiation of Mongolian shamans where they merge with the spirits and climb trees. Once I found myself standing halfway up a hill, at the top, emerging out of thin air was a great body of water which flowed powerfully past me. I stood by calmly watching and found I was standing next to a tree. Then the spirits merged with me and I found myself climbing up and down the tree repeatedly and rapidly with great ease. I realised this was the World Tree and flowing by, was the World River. This experience closely mirrors that of the Mongolian shamans and was undoubtedly an initiation.

Although I have the utmost respect for the ancient lineages, there were at some point the first shamans, the ones with no teachers, the ones finding their way alone through the great conversation with the universe. The newly awakening western shamans are finding themselves in this position. As Josephine Fire Lame Deer says,

'those with the spiritual strength to walk in ceremony-way but with no teachers from childhood, must find their own way with the help of the spirits.'

Often, inside indigenous cultures 'shaman' or its equivalent is a title bestowed on the person by a community that recognises what they are. Outside of these cultural parameters it's just a word but I would argue it's a word we need to use because it's highly unlikely that western society is going to start awarding this title. The community in which I live, doesn't know what a shaman is, and if they did, they probably wouldn't want one! Rather than the title I prefer to use the word shaman to describe a specific spiritual condition. This is a condition that may result in one that is not only a technician of the sacred but also a spiritual ecologist, one who through direct experience can articulate the intelligence of nature and the importance of maintaining balance. Siberian shamans talk of 'ongon hirbee daida', the sacred land, a phrase acknowledging that,

> *'...the land is sacred because it is inhabited by the spirits of the ancestors and the nature spirits who protect and maintain the ecology of the natural world.' 39*

Traditional peoples have followed this way of spiritual ecology for thousands of years and have managed to live harmoniously in the world with little or no detrimental impact. The main problems affecting the world today are the product of western culture and change must come from within that culture if we are to return to any form of balanced state on this planet. This is why shamanic people are appearing in the west. Perhaps they will act like a spiritual virus destroying the system from within. In his book, 'Shamans Through Time-500 Years on the Path to Knowledge', Jeremy Narby points out that there has been, *'...a great flowering of neo-shamanism...these neo-shamans have barely been studied.'* This is an important point and I suspect that if such a study were to be undertaken it might be discovered that some of these new western shamans have undergone spiritual awakening phenomena that bear a great similarity to traditional models.

The new western shamanism needs to offer a balanced alternative to counteract both the extremes of religious fundamentalism and the rise of fundamentalist atheism. A true spiritual awakening automatically changes the way the individual acts in the world. We consider in a different way, how we earn our living, where our food comes from, how our actions affect our community and the planet. It cannot be denied that within some traditional shamanisms there are practices designed to cause harm to other beings. Clearly this type of shamanism is not what she should aspire to in seeking a better world. I feel we need a shamanism, where the highest enlightening principles, combine with earth-based spirituality. This, in combination with movements like permaculture and deep ecology, creates a powerful, practical spirituality.

Although in some traditional societies the shaman receives payment, I do not think this a model that modern western shamans should follow. It is only right to pay for crafted shamanic tools like drums and rattles, or to be taught techniques of yoga and meditation, this is a tangible exchange. However, the proliferation of courses, clients, and price-lists for intangible spiritual services, is something that personally I am uncomfortable with. Whilst there are of course some genuine people out there, much of what is being sold as shamanism today, is little more than psychology with a veneer of spirituality. I know that this point of view will make me unpopular with many but charging for the intangible is really no different to the mediaeval church charging for indulgences. In thirteenth century France, Catharism emerged as a real threat to the church simply by returning to a pure form of Christianity and embodying an ideal of the original apostolic life. This included equal status for women in religious life and living in spiritual poverty. That they were in alignment with a greater truth is evidenced by the fact that the church instigated a crusade against them lasting forty years that was so barbaric it became the first genocide in Europe. Better to be like the Cathars than the church, I think. Many people do like to give something in order to receive and I have no issue with this. I have for example, been gifted magic mushrooms in honey and handmade shamanic objects in exchange for my time and this sits well with me. However, there seems to me, to be a sort of dark magic in the energy of actual money, worry of its lack lurks as fear, at the back of so many minds, and commercialisation of the sacred only serves to consolidate its hold.

In France the traditional healers are called *guérisseur* and there are two in my village. They are not shamans but *copeurs de feu*, meaning they can 'cut' fire. They can take away the pain from burns and skin diseases and do not even have to be physically present to effect the healing. Often the nurses from the hospital will call, unofficially, and simply give the name of a burn patient. Usually, within twenty minutes, the pain is gone. They also effectively treat cancer patients that have suffered burns through chemotherapy. These two women are actually the local hairdressers and elderly people from the old folks home come to get their hair done and any skin problems cured as a matter of course. They refuse to accept a penny for any healings, they earn a living by cutting hair. Having experienced what I have, I would not dare consider charging money for that which was gifted freely. How can we place monetary value on the soul?

Although there is great emphasis on the role of the shaman as a healer, some are primarily mystical visionaries and dreamers, those that can receive, interpret and pass on the great loving dream of the universe to those simply willing to listen. For my own part I fall primarily into this latter category and do not consider myself in any way a healer in the sense of a curandero for example. If someone asks me to drum for them, I will of course oblige, but the healing may come in ways that the person may not expect. Once a young woman to whom I'd taught some kundalini yoga meditation requested a healing session and so I drummed for her. She enjoyed it and felt a sense of well-being but nothing extraordinary. That night however I received a very big dream for her. I saw the woman and her boyfriend standing in a bathroom, symbolic of a place of purification. He is a gardener with a very deep connection to the earth, in the dream he was dressed as a shaman. The woman was holding a shoulder bag and there were two chrysalis stuck to it, one for each person. In front of them a giant dragonfly spanned the length of the room. The dragonfly lives the first part of its life underwater before emerging above into its true magnificence and is therefore a powerful symbol of transformation. This woman has very strong bhakti and from the dream I could tell her that, within the bag, she had all the tools needed for her own great transformation, everything was within her and ready. In Mongolian shamanism there is a word, 'butar', which means cocoon. They use this to describe a person that has the potential to become a shaman but is not answering the call. They have cocooned themselves and are not surrendering to the beautiful possibilities offered to them. That her boyfriend was dressed in shamanic costume told me the second chrysalis was for him and that he had the potential to become a shaman but did not realise this. They were delighted to receive this information as they were setting off to start a new life with all the uncertainty that entails. The dream was the real healing from the drumming, but how can you charge for a dream?

Yoga also, has not been immune to commercialisation, in fact yoga is big business. More often than not it is reduced to being nothing more than a glorified keep-fit regime, its original purpose of union with the Divine through the awakening of kundalini, forgotten. Kundalini yoga is very popular, with a large following. If you pay approximately five thousand U.S dollars you can qualify as a kundalini yoga teacher in under a month. There is absolutely no guarantee however, that two hundred hours of yoga will awaken a person's kundalini. Whilst there is much of value in kundalini yoga, the fact is, that the majority of kundalini yoga teachers are not kundalini awakened, and the qualification means nothing in this context, as they are teaching techniques designed to cultivate a spiritual condition of which they themselves have no comprehension. Kundalini yoga is a beautiful system for health and happiness but if kundalini awakening is your motivation to do yoga, bear in mind that being kundalini awakened is not a required prerequisite to be a kundalini yoga teacher. The Sanskrit texts are available free to all on the Internet and everything you need to know about the yoga of kundalini awakening is in the Hatha Yoga Pradapika and the Yoga Kundalini Upanishad.

It is true that a shaman must be chosen by the spirits and that you can't do a course or pay for this kind of initiation. But that doesn't mean you cannot become a shaman if your spiritual desire is strong enough. You must simply alter your state of consciousness so that the shamanic spirits want to be with you, want to choose you. I'm not saying don't get a spiritual qualification if you want to, I'm saying don't attribute any degree of spiritual authority to a piece of paper awarded by any human agency. This power is in all of us; we do not have to give our personal spiritual authority away to any other human being. Ultimately, success is guaranteed once we have taken our first steps on the spiritual path although it is the work of lifetimes. A wise yogi once said to me,

'we are all like fruit hanging from the Tree of Life, when we are ripe, we cannot but fail to fall, into the waiting hands of God.'

I share a great many dreams in this narrative. The Upanishads talk frequently about the three states of consciousness, waking, dreaming and deep sleep. Above these is the witness state turiya, ever present yet separate from all. In that context, dreams are considered merely a reflection of our concerns and desires in waking life and ultimately as unreal as waking life itself. However we are allowed one desire, that is spiritual desire and once our bhakti becomes focused this is reflected in our dreams, which then transcend the mundane and become agents of spirit.

The three shamanic worlds, themselves containing other worlds are a like a multiple layered dream interacting with our waking dream. Once I dreamed of a girl I know called Aishling. This very beautiful name means 'dream', in Irish. Within my dream, I had a dream of her; she gave me the message that we are all one. Still within my dream I woke up and went to find her and told her about the dream. The next day I met her and found myself telling a girl whose name means 'dream', about a dream, I had about her, in a dream. As my dream of the dancing shaman child showed me, we live in a world where our leaders are beyond influence, unreachable and untouchable by conventional methods, their power is consolidated by the corporations and the vast military complex. All we can do is that shaman dance, change our consciousness, and make sure our individual dreams within the collective dream reflect the highest truth.

I felt guided to share these experiences and I'm very glad I did because I find they reveal the great beauty of the way the Divine will express itself if you only let the Mother take your hand. I also gained a great deal of understanding by revisiting these memories, of messages and wisdom I was receiving but that were beyond me at the time. I share them not only for their beauty but also that others experiencing the phenomena of kundalini or shamanic awakenings may be helped by reading this account. Because the understanding of the shamanic spiritual awakening process has been forgotten in the west we no longer have our own words that meaningfully describe the condition of shaman. We do however have shamanic archetypes like Merlin, the Green Man and Mad Sweeney. These characters are of the forest and there is a certain wild quality about them. Becoming 'wild' certainly has been an aspect of my personal shamanic process. These wild archetypes give a sense of being apart from the community and I, for the most part, remain solitary. What I describe here is also in a sense, a shamanic 'Way of the Wildman', the shamanic way of the Sasquatch, Almas and Omé Pelut. Civilisation is what brought us away from this aspect of ourselves. The growth of cities meant the necessity for intensive agriculture. Wherever we find this, we find a pyramidical structure to society which persists to this day which essentially results in a tiny percentage of privileged few and the rest of us as slaves. Europeans lived as shamanic hunter-gatherers until the 'civilised' ones came bringing agriculture with them. The shamanic peoples of the world had no need to build temples, nature was its own temple. Likewise the sages that composed the Upanishads, removed themselves into nature. Despite the fact that India was no stranger to the rise and fall of great civilisations the sages sought and taught enlightenment in forest academies. One of the main Upanishads is called 'Brihadaranyaka', which means, 'of the great forest'.

I sense that there is an important message in these communications I received from the Sasquatch and the Almas, that although we are clearly a different type of animal to all others on this planet, we are deeply connected to these Wild

People and that they want us to remember this. I believe that they are the original hominids of this planet and that rather than having evolved from them we have somehow been created from them. The Yokuts have a beautiful story of how the animals created people. Each animal suggested an attribute and it was Hairy Man that said, *people should walk on two legs like me.* This is saying that Hairy Man gave part of himself to us. We need to remember this because we have a choice. We can go fully with civilisation or we can balance it by reconnecting with our ancient Sasquatch/Alma selves, bring forth that part of us that is the natural shaman-yogi of this planet. Peoples with surviving shamanic cultures still know this. Trainee curanderos may spend years alone in the jungle dieting plants, in this way the forest literally becomes alive to them. In the north west of Canada, the Squamish sent their shamans to be out alone into the wilderness for up to ten years. In this way they returned to their wild selves. They had to be re-found and re-integrated into society along with the knowledge they had gained. In the pictograph at Painted Rock, Hairy Man is crying. This is because of the way that human beings became in the world. The problem is that we worship the great minds but not the great hearts. We need to bring this into balance and make Hairy Man stop crying.

It is clear that the Way of the Human is currently not beneficial to our beautiful planet, and now that we are venturing into outer space we are bringing the same problems with us; our concerns being primarily about plundering our planetary neighbours for natural resources and dividing up territories, we hear little about the ecological conservation of the Moon or Mars. Despite the best efforts of our governments to suppress information and ridicule or intimidate witnesses, the evidence overwhelmingly points to the conclusion that we are not alone in the universe and that our responsibilities therefore extend beyond this planet. The search for extraterrestrial civilisation remains focused on finding material evidence but there is most certainly also a spiritual element to the UFO phenomenon. Initially, I wasn't going to include anything about UFOs here but a vision of flying saucers coming towards me, whilst a spirit opened a book, caused me to reconsider. UFOs have been a subtle spiritual presence throughout my process. In the early days of my kundalini awakening, I dreamed of a UFO sending down blue lightening. In another dream, a UFO inverted itself into a chalice containing a blue liquid that was poured into my heart. The colour blue in the dreams caused me to identify these UFOs with Shiva. Another time I dreamed of two huge flying saucers, resting motionless in the sky above our field. This felt so real that I was sure I would see them in ordinary reality, but they never came. I related earlier, how just before taking *amanita muscaria*, I was shown a UFO and told, *THIS is the big meditation*.

In dreams I have also encountered beings that I sensed strongly were from other planets. Once I met a group of very tall blond 'people', dressed in white futuristic clothes. One of them, who was about nine feet tall, bent down and picked me up. He said, ah, *an enlivened one! Do you know what that means? Let me show you.* He carried me to a pure white room where we lay down to sleep but I remember nothing after. Another time I met a female of the same kind with a jewel on her forehead, she was presiding over an operation on a human. I wasn't happy about this but she said it was necessary.

My sense is that at least some of the UFOs are inter-dimensional and that they may occupy the same places between the worlds that shamans also frequent. Once, Michèle and I were walking in a field, when she spotted an unusual plant and bent down to examine it. At the exact moment she was looking down, I was looking up. Only a few metres above me, a bright gleaming metal object appeared out of nowhere and shot across the sky for a short distance before vanishing into thin air. What I saw was very close to me and I sensed it was part of something bigger, as if just its edge had slipped briefly into this dimension. It all happened so fast, that by the time Michèle looked up from the plant, it was over and she found me standing there in open-mouthed amazement.

It is sometimes suggested that the UFO abduction experience may be the modern minds interpretation of the traditional shamanic initiation by spirits. Or, that in fact the aliens were the 'spirits' all along. There are certainly parallels to be drawn between the operations performed on abductees and the dismemberments experienced by shamans. Likewise, abductees report having implants inserted in them and shamans have objects like crystals put inside them. However, many indigenous people have legends of Star People and in India, the flying ships known as vimanas, are well documented in the Sanskrit texts. Flying saucers are also a common theme in the ayahuasca art of visionary Amazonian shamans. It is clear to me, that historically shamans have certainly been aware of UFOs and their occupants, yet have not confused them with their shamanic spirits. Another thing is that shamans remember their initiatory experiences whereas abductees report missing time and the memory of the event may not emerge until hypnotic regression takes place. That said, there is no denying that many abductees become spiritualized after their experiences, so perhaps the abduction phenomenon is to do with making a different kind of shaman.

A very intriguing link between UFOs and shamanism is the presence of owls. This has been explored in depth by Mike Clelland in his book, *The Messengers: Owls, Synchronicity and the UFO Abductee*, in which some of my own experiences feature. One night I dreamed I was standing with a white owl, high on a hill, overlooking a valley. Shortly after this, a tawny owl and a barn owl came together in a dream, the barn owl nuzzled my hand. The following night I awoke into a vision of the oak tree that stands in our field. Its leaves and branches were enveloping me, pulling at me urgently. I had the sense it wanted me to go outside, and even though it was about four o'clock in the morning, I pulled myself out of bed and answered the call. Outside, owls were calling, Orion was above me, and to the left, a planet shone as bright as a moon. I had only a few seconds to take in the glory of this, when what I'd thought was a star, flew upwards across the sky with a snake-like movement. I have no doubt that this was a UFO and that the tree had called me out to see it.

From my own perspective however, it is the shaman and the tree that are intrinsically connected. The shaman is in essence the human embodiment of the tree, the shaman's connection is very much to the Earth, and although I may look in wonder to the stars, I know that here, is home.

Many shamanic traditions believe that the soul may split apart usually due to various shocks or traumas experienced in life. In order to restore wholeness, shamans conduct soul retrievals, journeying to the other worlds to bring back the missing parts. With me, soul parts often manifest as tiny birds. There was a time when I was feeling a lot of fear and unease, so I asked to find the source of this within myself. I entered a very dingy, gloomy room, with dirty brown walls and peeling wallpaper. In this place I found two beautiful birds, one was a jay, which flew up into my hands. I took it outside and released it into the sky. I went back in and found the other bird, I picked it up and found its wings were broken and I felt responsible for this. When I threw it into the air, it hung motionless for a few moments and I was afraid it might fall but then it began slowly to flap its wings with increasing power. As it rose into the sky, the wings became bigger and bigger until it was like an eagle flying up to the Heavens. Our wings are never truly broken. After releasing these beautiful soul parts back to Oneness, all my fear simply left me.

Once I came out of a very deep meditation and found myself in a shocking situation. I didn't know where I was, how I was, who I was or what I was; I was utterly alone, there was only energy. This state passed after a few moments but made me think about the universe. The Vedas tell us that the One Soul, in order to experience itself fully in divine play (lila), divided itself into the illusion of infinitesimal separation, that the universe exists purely for the purpose of concealing and revealing the divinity of the Oneness from and to itself. Perhaps the One Soul shattered itself out of shock and loneliness. Sometimes, during a soul retrieval, a soul-part may return willingly to oneness but others are just not ready to return at that time. So it goes with us and God, and as such, the universe may be viewed as one giant cosmic exercise in soul retrieval, our purpose as fragments of the One, is to find our way home.

Years after my initial awakening I ask, *who am I? why am I here?* I'm given a vision, I see the air full of golden molecules that coalesce into the form of a jaguar. Spirits throw the jaguar up into a tree. Jaguar-me begins to climb. In another vision I see the shamanic anaconda and the kundalini king cobra. They are entwined in a DNA helix, like ida and pingala nadis, like the oscillating souls of the Siberian shamans. I caress their heads and they slide fluidly through my hands out into the cosmos, serpents of shamanism and yoga in complimentary balance. In a dream I find myself like the little snail in the story finding his way home. First, I am in my childhood home and I know I am going on a journey. In front of me is a large key ring with dozens of keys. I call my father to ask which are the right keys for the next place I am going, Coolinarne, the Land of the Sloe Trees. This is the home of my Irish ancestors and a second home to me. Eventually I find myself approaching a sacred mound in the woods, the home of my ancient Sasquatch/Almas self. The road is very muddy but I don't mind because where I am going is beautiful. Then, as I'm walking, something comes up behind me and very lightly and gently grabs my legs. I spin around to see my Siamese cat, Singha, a little bodhisattva, running away mischievously across a field to a dry stone wall, just like the one where I found the statue of Isis in my dream. I see that over the wall is my current home in France, Anma, which means 'soul' in Occitan. I then realise that I have been given all the keys I need and that whether I take the way of yoga straight across the field, or the shamanic path through the woods, I am going HOME.

On this journey home, the influences in my shamanic path have come from diverse cultures. Yet the lessons I received were universal and I applied them to who I was and where I was. I discovered kundalini in the Gaelic harp, I used the technique of 'dieting' from Peru to reconnect with druidic knowledge, the trees and entheogens of Ireland and France showed me their medicine, I made drums from animals and trees that have a strong connection to my land and culture. We should not think of shamanism as something that happens somewhere else, it happens in the centre, which is always within you, wherever you are.

The English composer Ralph Vaughan Williams, upon first discovering English folk music said that he felt a sense of recognition, of something he had always known, yet hadn't known was there. He said,

> *'a folksong is like a tree, whose stem dates back from immemorial times, but which continually puts out new shoots. In one aspect the folksong is as old as time itself; in another aspect it is no older than the singer who sang it'. 40*

We can also rediscover that which has always been there, waiting patiently for us to remember and become new shoots of shamanism, new singers of the oldest song.

CHAPTER TWENTY-SIX
A SHAMANIC KUNDALINI UPANISHAD

There is only one soul, this is the Spirit within all things

The essence of this Spirit is Love

You are that Spirit within all things.

It is this One that looks out of every eye be it grasshopper or great whale

It is this One that knows the heat of the sun as mineral or tree,

Through every aspect of creation this One Spirit knows itself

There are two aspects to the Great Spirit

She that creates the Sacred Illusion and He that experiences

These aspects are not separate but one

Duality and Oneness exist together in the Great Mystery

Know you are the One by going to the forest

There, in meditation journey with the spirits of the animals and plants

Let them reveal to you the illusion of your separation from them and all that is

With your drum remember the heart beat of the mother

Sit in meditation and know Her as the serpent, like the serpent move softly on the earth and shed your skin

Sitting with spine erect be fearless like the jaguar

Let the anaconda swim up the spine as the salmon up the waterfall returning to source

On the wings of the condor you will remember who you are

Know that the anaconda, jaguar and condor are one

Feel the legs of the cosmic spider dancing at the fontanel as you enter the unitive state

The cosmic spider pours forth the web of creation from within itself, then rests within this web at its centre

As both container and contained, aware of all activity within its web, the Great Spirit remains untouched, unensnared.

Realise the unitive state of stillness in activity, do no harm, only through a loving life can Love be known

The wise know the universe as unlimited manifestation and possibility in eternal unchanging consciousness

You are That

This is the Upanishad

Om shanti shanti shanti

BIBLIOGRAPHY

Allegro, John M. The Sacred Mushroom and the Cross. Hodder and Stoughton, 1970. Armstrong, Robert Bruce. The Irish and Highland Harps. Irish University Press, New impression edition, 1970.

Beyer, Stephen V. Singing to the Plants-A Guide to Mestizo Shamanism in the Upper Amazon. University of New Mexico Press, 2009.

Breeze Wood, Nicholas. Sacred Drums of Siberia. Nicholas Breeze Wood, 2013.

Campbell, John. The Inner Reaches of Outer Space -Metaphor as Myth and as Religion. New World Library 2012.

De la Rubio Muñoz and Dr. Myra Shackley. Wildmen: Yeti, Sasquatch and the Neanderthal Enigma. London: Thames and Hudson, 1983.

Eliade, Mircea. Shamanism -Archaic Techniques of Ecstacy. Princeton University Press.

Ferguson, Susan. The Matrix and the Sanskrit Texts.

Ferguson, Susan. Shimmering Snakes of Light in the Time Before Forgetting.

Gaup, Ailo. The Shamanic Zone. Nittedal, Three Bears Publishing, 2005.

Harner, Michael. Way of the Shaman. Harper and Row, 1980.

Ingerman, Sandra and Hank Wesselman. Awakening to the Spirit World -The Shamanic Path of Direct Revelation. Boulder, Sounds True, 2010.

Joseph Epes Brown, ed. The Sacred Pipe Black Elk's Account of the Seven Rites of the Oglala Sioux. University of Oklahoma Press, 1953.

Krishna, Gopi. The Awakening of Kundalini. New York, E.P. Dutton and Co. 1975.

Krishna, Gopi. Kundalini in Time and Space. New Delhi, The Kundalini Research Publication Trust 1979

Krishna, Gopi. The Real Nature of Mystical Experience. New Delhi, The Kundalini Research Publication Trust, 1979.

Krishna, Gopi. The Secret of Yoga. New York, Harper and Row 1972.

Liesowska, Anna. Siberian Times-Is this the worlds oldest secret code? 22nd October 2014.

London, Jack. Martin Eden. The MacMillan Company 1909.

London, Jack. The Call of the Wild. Heritage Illustrated Publishing 2014.

Manker, Ernst. Zaubertrommel I – II

Manning, David. Vaughan Williams on Music. Oxford University Press 2007.

Meyer, Lauren. Sami Noaidi and Inuit Angakoq: Traditional Shamanic Roles and Practices.

McKenna, Terence. Food of the Gods. New York, Bantam Books, 1992.

Moore, Jerry. D. Visions of Culture: An Introduction to Anthropological Theories and Theorists. AltaMira Press 2012.

D. Mortenson. Peru's Top Indigenous Leader Says Industry, Traffickers Behind Shaman Slayings, Truthout.

Moskowitz Strain, Kathy. Mayak Datat: The Hairy Man Pictographs. The Relict Homonoid Inquiry 1:1-12, 2012.

Narby, Jeremy. The Cosmic Serpent DNA and the Origins of Knowledge. New York, Penguin, 1998.

Narby, Jeremy. Shamans Through Time: 500 Years on the Path to Knowledge. Tarcher 2012.

Neihardt, John. G. Black Elk Speaks-The Complete Edition. University of Nebraska Press, 1932.

Nikhilananda, S. trans. The Gospel of Sri Ramakrishna. New York, Ramakrishna-Vivekenanda Centre, 1942.

O'Curry, Eugene. On the Manners and Customs of the Ancient Irish. Williams and Norgate, 1873.

The Rig Veda. Trans. Ralph T. H. Griffith. Kotagiri (Nilgiri), 1896.

Sanger, Keith and Alison Kinnaird. Tree Of Strings: Crann Nan Tued: A History of the Harp in Scotland. Kilmore Music, 1992.

Sarangarel. Chosen by the Spirits Following Your Shamanic Calling. Vermont, Destiny Books.

Sarangarel. Riding Windhorses A Journey into the Heart of Mongolian Shamanism. Vermont, Destiny Books.

Schultes, Richard Evans, Albert Hofmann and Christian Rätsch. Plants of the Gods-Their Sacred, Healing and Hallucinogenic Powers. Inner Traditions 2001.

Sri Amneon, Gavin. Serpent Vine on the Tree Spine. School of Mysticism, Melbourne Australia 2012.

Svatmarama, Swami. The Hatha Yoga Pradaprika. Trans. Brian Dana Akers. New York: YigaVidya.com, 2002.

The Upanishads. Trans. Eknath Easwaran. Niligri Press, 1987.

Wasson, R. Soma-Divine Mushroom of Immortality. 1967

Wilcox, Joan Parisi. Masters of the Living Energy The Mystical World of the Q'ero of Peru. Inner Traditions 1999.

Wood, J. 'Snakes' seen in human cells. phys.org

Yajurveda, Krishna. Yoga Kundalini Upanishad. Trans. Thakur Krishna Uprety. Kathmandu: Divine Yoga Institute, 2015.

Yogani. Advanced Yoga Practice-Easy Lessons for Ecstatic Living.

RECOMMENDED INTERNET RESOURCES

Ayahuasca Forums-forums.ayahuasca.com

Cumha https://youtu.be/s0gM-5VRm3I

http://www.dreamglade.com

Erowid-www.erowid.org

Irish Icaro https://youtu.be/t-2nnSJ2Z8E

Mastery of Meditation, Yoga and Zen-anmolmehta.com

Metaphysical Musing-www.metaphysicalmusing.com

Sami Culture www.utexas.edu

Shamanic Community (Facebook group)

http://hiddenexperience.blogspot.fr/

TheKundaliniYoga.Org-www.thekundaliniyoga.org

www.bigfootencounters.com

http://www.thewayinn.com

GLOSSARY OF SPIRITUAL TERMINOLOGY

- Agua florida-Cologne used widely in the Amazon for purification, cleansing and healing.

- Ajna chakra-Sanskrit, ‘control’. The sixth chakra, known as the third eye.

- Ajos sacha-Mansoa alliace, ‘False garlic’, commonly used for plant baths in the Amazon.

- Almas-Mongolian, ‘wild-man’. Perhaps a surviving population of homo erectus.

- *Amanita muscaria*-Entheogenic mushroom containing the psychoactive, muscimol.

- Amaroli-Yogic practice of urine drinking.

- Amrita-Sanskrit, ‘nectar’. Mysterious spiritual secretions produced in the brain of a kundalini-awakened person that drip down through the nasal pharynx.

- Anma-Occitan, meaning soul.

- Asana-A yoga posture.

- Ayahuasca-Banisteriopsis caapi, a South American jungle vine used in combination with other plants in the entheogenic brew of the same name.

- Bhakti-Focused spiritual desire.

- Bindu chakra-Located at the back of the head, this chakra is associated with the production of ‘amrita’.

- Bitwi-An African religion centred around the powerful entheogen, iboga.

- Bodhisattva-An enlightened being or one seeking enlightenment, for the sake of all sentient beings.

- Bodhrán-Irish frame drum.

- Buryats-The largest indigenous group in Siberia.

- Catharism-An alternative Christianity that flourished in Southern France in the thirteenth century.

- Chacruna-Pyscohotria viridis, a plant containing a high percentage of DMT and one of the principle components of the ayahuasca brew.

- Chaliponga-Diplopterys cabrerana, a plant containing a higher percentage of DMT than chacruna, sometimes used instead of the latter in the ayahuasca brew.

- Clairseach-The Irish wire-strung harp.

- Comhluighe-Irish Gaelic, two strings of equal pitch on the clairseach, symbolising the lying together of divine masculine and feminine.

- Cumha-Irish Gaelic, melancholic separation.

- Chakra-Sanskrit, 'wheel'. Spiritual energy centres in the subtle body.

- Curandero-'Healer', a traditional term for an Amazonian shaman.

- Dieta-A restrictive diet used by Amazonian shamans to bond with the spirit of a particular plant and for healing.

- DMT-Dimethyltryptamine, a psychedelic compound of the tryptamine family.
- Enlightenment-In yogic terms, the blending of an awakened kundalini with inner silence.
- Entheogen-'That which awakens the god within'. A preferable term to 'drug', when referring to teacher plants.
- Gol-Buryat word for the shamanic concept of the 'centre', the meeting of all possibilities, places and time.
- Govadas-Sami shamanic drum.
- Hairy Man-Yokut Indian name for Bigfoot.
- Huachuma-A traditional name for San Pedro cactus.
- Ida nadi-One of the three main energy channels in the subtle body, it has a lunar aspect.
- Icaros-Healing songs sung by Amazonian shamans during ayahuasca ceremonies.
- Isis-Egyptian goddess of rebirth.
- Kechari mudra-Sanskrit, 'to fly through space'. The practice of raising the tongue to the nasal pharynx, allowing ecstatic energy to flow between the pelvis and the head.
- Kundalini-Sanskrit, 'coiled'. Divine feminine spiritual energy, residing at the base of the human spine.
- Nadis-Spiritual energy channels in the subtle body.
- Kriya-Automatic yoga movements experienced by a kundalini awakened person.

- Lila-Divine ‘play’, the experience of Shiva in the illusion of separation.
- Limpieza-A spiritual cleaning.
- Manomani-Sanskrit, ‘bridge’.
- Mantra-Sanskrit, ‘mind-tool’. Sacred syllable or syllables used to induce deep meditation.
- Mareado-Means ‘dizzy’, term used to describe the effects of ayahuasca.
- Maya-Sanskrit, ‘illusion’.
- Mescaline -The psychedelic component in San Pedro cactus.
- Muscimol -The psychoactive constituent of amanita muscaria
- Noaide-Sami shaman.
- Non-Ordinary Reality-(NOR), a phrase coined by Michael Harner to denote the other realities experienced in shamanic states of consciousness.
- Om-The primal first sound of the universe.
- Omé pelut-Occitan word to describe a Wild Person, meaning ‘hairy man’.
- Ongon-Siberian shamanic term for an object that represents or houses the spirits.
- Ordinary Reality-(OR), a term coined by Michael Harner, to describe the state of consciousness through which we normally perceive the world.

- Pingala nadi-One of the three main energy channels in the subtle body, it has a solar aspect.

- Psilocybin-The psychedelic compound in 'magic' mushrooms.

- Sahasrara-The crown chakra.

- Samadhi-Sanskrit, absorption in pure consciousness.

- Samhain-Irish Gaelic, a festival marking the end of the harvest and the beginning of winter. The origin of Halloween.

- San Pedro-Trichocereus pachanoi, psychoactive cactus containing mescaline

- Sasquatch-From Salish, Sésquac meaning 'wild-man'.

- Shakti-Sanskrit, 'primal power'. Awakened kundalini, the dynamic divine feminine creative force in human beings and the universe.

- Shaktipat-Transference of kundalini energy from guru to disciple.

- Shaman-Originally from Tunguskan, saman, 'one who knows'.

- Shamanism-Archaic techniques of ecstasy, including drumming, dancing and ingestion of certain plants, in order to induce altered states of consciousness, enter the spirit worlds and effect change on behalf of the community.

- Soma-A god and a plant. Also, a substance produced in the gastro-intestinal tract of a kundalini-awakened body.

- Sushumna-The most important spiritual channel in the subtle body. Corresponding to the spine, it the path of kundalini from root to crown chakra.

- Sutra Neti-A yogic purification, involving passing a cord through the nasal passage and pulling it out of the mouth.

- Sunsii mur-Buryat, ‘Trail of Spirit’. A stream of consciousness, linking all shamans

- Syrian rue-Perganum harmala, a plant sometimes identified as soma and used in ayahuasca analogues.

- Tabernanthe iboga-This very powerful entheogen, is a rainforest shrub from Central West Africa, the psychoactive component being ibogaine.

- Tantra-Sanskrit, ‘woven together’, the most all-encompassing system of yoga.

- Therianthrope-A being that is part animal, part human.

- Three Worlds-The Upper, Lower and Middle worlds, acknowledged in some form by many shamanic traditions.

- Tobacco-Nicotiana rustica, known in South America as mapacho.

- Toé-brugmansia suaveolens, one of the most powerful plants used in Amazonian shamanism, the visionary component being the alkaloid, scopolamine

- Turiya-The eternal, unchanging, witnessing consciousness, represented by the dot at the top of the Om symbol.

- Udha-Buryat, the principle spirit bonded to a shaman. Upanishads-Sanskrit, ‘to draw closer’. An important collection of Vedic texts.

- Wild-People-Collective term used her referring to the cryptid hominids of the planet e.g. Sasquatch, Yeti, Almas, omé pelut, Yeren, Yowi ect.

- Yoga-Sanskrit, ‘union’. A vast body of spiritual practices, aiming towards spiritual evolution.

NOTES

1. G.Krishna *Secrets of Kundalini in Pamchastavi*
2. G.Krishna *Kundalini in Time and Space*
3. G.Krishana *The Mystery of the Coiled Serpent*
4. M.Eliade *Shamanism*
5. Ibid
6. Ibid
7. A.Liesowska *Siberian Times*
8. Ibid
9. Eliade *Shamanism*
10. J.Campbell *The Inner Reaches of Outer Space*
11. Ibid
12. J.Parisi Wilcox *Masters of the Living energy*
13. *The Yoga Kundalini Upanishad*
14. *The Hatha Yoga Pradpika*
15. Ibid
16. Ibid
17. Ibid
18. Ibid

19. Ibid

20. Ibid

21. C. Shaw *The Silent Ecocide*

22. Ibid

23. J. Narby *The Cosmic Serpent*

24. Ibid

25. Ibid

26. J.Wood *'Snakes' seen in human cells, phys. Org*

27. Sarangerel *Riding Windhorses*

28. S.Ferguson *Shimmering Snakes of Light in the Time Before Forgetting*

29. Sarangerel *Chosen by the Spirits*

30. J.Campbell *The Inner Reaches of Outer Space*

31. E.O'Curry *Manners and Customs of the Ancient Irish*

32. A. Gaup *The Shamanic Zone*

33. JD. Moore *Visions of Culture*

34. Ibid

35. Sarangerel *Chosen by the Spirits*

36. *The Hatha Yoga Pradpika*

37. www.bigfootencounters.com

38. JE.Brown *The Sacred Pipe*

39. Sarangerel *Chosen by the Spirits*

40. D.Manning *Vaughan Williams on Music*

14774955R00140

Printed in Great Britain
by Amazon.co.uk, Ltd.,
Marston Gate.